THE PRICE OF GOLD

THE PRICE OF GOLD

The Toll and the Triumph of
One Man's Olympic Dream

MARTY NOTHSTEIN
WITH IAN DILLE

RODALE.

For my team

Rodale books may be purchased for business or promotional use or for special sales. For information, please write to: Special Markets Department, Rodale, Inc., 733 Third Avenue, New York, NY 10017

Printed in the United States of America
Rodale Inc. makes every effort to use acid-free ♾, recycled paper ♺.

Book design by Christopher Rhoads

Library of Congress Cataloging-in-Publication Data

Nothstein, Marty.
    The price of gold : the toll and the triumph of one man's Olympic dream / Marty Nothstein with Ian Dille.
        p.   cm.
    ISBN 978–1–60961–337–2 hardcover
    1. Nothstein, Marty.   2. Cyclists—United States—Biography.
    3. Olympic athletes—United States—Biography.   I. Dille, Ian.   II. Title.
    GV1051.N67A3   2012
796.6'2092—dc23
[B]   2012006435

Distributed to the trade by Macmillan
2   4   6   8   10   9   7   5   3   1   hardcover

We inspire and enable people to improve their lives and the world around them.

CONTENTS

ACKNOWLEDGMENTS

Marty

The decision to tell my own story in print did not come easily. I realized that recounting my life's events, as I experienced them, might result in some objections by the individuals involved. Additionally, I knew that I would have to speak candidly, and sometimes critically, about myself.

But I did not make the decision to share my story alone. Nor does my life's story belong to only me. I owe a large debt of gratitude to those that made the production of this book, and the story held within, possible.

Heidi Rodale believed my story should exist in the published world, and remained determined to make it a reality.

The support of my wife, Christi, was invaluable, as always. Her willingness to share intimate moments from our lives made this book significantly more genuine.

My kids, Tyler and Devon, are my constant inspiration.

I count my family—my parents, Gail and Wayne, and my siblings Tim, Carlene, Waynette, and Jay—amongst my biggest fans, and I, theirs. My family's influence on my life is a primary reason this book is about winning a gold medal.

Gil Hatton never forgets a good story (even those I wish he would), and his skill as an oral historian of the sport greatly contributed to this book.

Erin Hartwell insisted that I tell my story as it actually happened, or not tell it at all. He is perhaps my most well-read friend, and I took his advice seriously.

My coauthor, Ian Dille, pulled me to the finish line and let me sprint across.

Finally, Air Products, the steadfast sponsor of T-Town's development programs, helped make my Olympic journey, as recounted in this book, possible.

Ian

The initial e-mail, describing the proposed book, was innocuous enough. The project that ensued was one requiring the accrued experience of a veteran book editor, working with a first-time author. Thank-you, Shannon Welch, for your editorial guidance, wealth of patience, and honest feedback.

Marty, thank-you for bringing me into your life, from past to present. (Thanks, too, for the lead out at the Thursday night training race during the research phase of the book. It's a rare honor to be shepherded upon The Blade's wheel.)

Lindy, my wife, thank-you for being a test audience of one—nodding your head when you listened to a section you liked, and crinkling your nose when you didn't. Your unvarnished critiques are one of the many reasons I love you so.

Annie Melton, how would I have possibly managed without your tireless and dedicated assistance? You have a bright future as a journalist. Go for it.

Only the world's proudest father would spend decades compiling boxes' worth of newspaper clippings about his son, and then hand it all over to a complete stranger. Thank-you, Wayne Nothstein.

Heidi Rodale, thank-you for carrying on your dad's legacy at T-Town.

Gil, you are truly the Bear.

Jack Simes, your insight was invaluable, thank-you.

Peter Flax and Bill Strickland, thank-you for recommending I write this book.

PART I

1

STONE MOUNTAIN

I'M 25 YEARS OLD when I arrive in Atlanta for the 1996 Olympic Games. I'm a world-class track cyclist at the peak of my physical prowess. I stand 6 feet 2 inches and weigh 225 pounds. My quads measure 30 inches around, the size of a normal cyclist's waistline. My shoulders, biceps, and chest appear Herculean in proportion to the svelte carbon-fiber bike I race. In the weight room I squat more than 500 pounds. In training, my explosive sprint, which tops out near 50 miles per hour, frequently demolishes bicycle parts.

I twist handlebars into pretzels and fold chainrings like pancakes.

I turn wheels into tacos.

I've taught the millions of muscle fibers in my legs to fire, so that I may ride a bike faster than any human on the planet.

The event in which I specialize, match sprinting, is the equivalent of the 100-meter dash, but on bikes. Two racers go head-to-head on the track over three laps, the last 200 meters of which is timed. The first one across the line moves on to the next round of the sprint tournament. The loser goes home. The gold medalist in the Olympic match sprint is considered the fastest cyclist in the world.

Tour de France racers sometimes go as fast as me. Down mountains.

But match sprinting isn't just about sheer speed. Winning a match-sprint tournament requires impeccable timing and tactics, and the ability to trade jabs and go blow for blow over a series of punishing rounds.

3

In Atlanta I'll face the fastest sprinters in the world—and the most cunning. It's a chess game followed by a boxing match.

. . . .

The chess game comes first. The race is three laps, but rarely is someone stupid enough to go all out from the gun. Your opponent would simply sit comfortably in your draft, conserving energy as you push through the wind, and zip by just before the finish line.

Instead, you wait. You and your opponent crawl around the track for the first lap. You size each other up. When is he going to make his move? When will I make my move? You glare menacingly at each other. It's an Old West shoot-out. Who'll draw first?

A random draw prior to the start determines who leads the race from the start line. Some riders want to lead the race. Others prefer to follow. The racers gauge their own strengths against their opponent's weaknesses. Then they determine whether to sprint from in front of, or from behind, their competitor. Sometimes both racers want to follow. They come to a complete standstill—a track stand—as each tries to force the other into taking the lead. These track stands can last minutes. Both riders balance motionless, in the middle of the race, until one cracks and assumes the lead.

Those who lead out a match sprint will ramp up their speed from a lap or more away from the finish and get going so fast that their competitor can't pass them. Or, they'll physically block their opponent from passing by swerving up and down the track, waiting until the last moment to sprint for the line—too late to be passed.

Those who follow are the assassins of match sprinting. They stalk their opponents from a distance. Then, on the last lap they'll sprint into their competitor's draft, and slingshot past, coming through the last corner, right before the finish line.

With my size and power, I've developed into a racer who likes to control the front of a match sprint. I keep a close eye on my opponent. I make sure he doesn't sneak by me. Then, with a clear line to the finish, I start my sprint. When I hit max speed, my competitor often implodes, giving up well before the finish line.

The winner of two out of three matches takes the round, and lives to race again.

· · · · · · · · ·

Leading up to the Atlanta Games, I'm the undeniable favorite. I announced my presence as the rider to beat at the 1994 world championships, where I won double gold in the match sprint and *keirin*, a race that simultaneously pits five sprinters against one another. In 1995 I took third at worlds in the team sprint, a three-man event, despite competing just months after fracturing my kneecap when a wheel collapsed underneath me in training.

During the 1996 season, I'm undefeated in both the match sprint and the keirin at the three World Cup events I've raced—an unrivaled feat.

I'm picked to win my event by nearly every major publication covering the Olympics, including *Sports Illustrated*. And I have absolutely no excuse not to dominate the competition here in Atlanta. With the Olympics on home soil, USA Cycling rolls out the red carpet.

In the years running up to the games, the international electronics corporation, Electronic Data Systems (EDS), and one of the world's top bike manufacturers, GT Bicycles, joined forces with USA Cycling. The result is Project '96. The goal is US gold medals in cycling events. Hundreds of thousands of dollars pour into the creation of a Superbike, utilizing state-of-the-art aerodynamic technology and wind-tunnel testing. The final product looks as sleek as a stealth bomber, painted in red, white, and blue.

GT knows the lightweight Superbike won't hold up under the power of my sprint, so the company flies engineers out to my home track in Trexlertown, Pennsylvania. They custom build numerous carbon-fiber prototypes. Finally, we develop the perfect sprinting machine. The bike is silver. I love it. It looks like a Porsche 911, only faster. I can't muscle a millimeter of flex out of the bike, but it doesn't ride like a tank, either. The bike dives up and down the Atlanta cycling track with unreal dexterity.

At the '96 Olympics, the cycling track, or velodrome, is 250 meters long, roughly half the size of a running track. Its corners are banked at 45 degrees to keep racers from flying up and over the edge of the turns (though they still sometimes do). If you sit at a top corner of the track you'll slide down the smooth wooden boards to the blue out-of-bounds apron ringing the inside.

The velodrome sits directly below Stone Mountain, a giant granite dome that rises from the earth 20 miles east of Atlanta. The huge rock soars more than 800 feet above a forest of Georgia oaks, and its base extends 9 miles underground. When I look out beyond the far end of the oval track, past turns three and four, I can see nothing but the looming Stone Mountain.

I don't need to travel far to get to the track. In Atlanta Jim Kennedy, of Cox Enterprises, a good friend of mine, puts the US Olympic cycling team up in a luxurious, sprawling compound, just a few minutes from the Stone Mountain velodrome. USA Cycling brings in Spago chefs to cook us meals. During our free time in the days preceding the Games, we chip golf balls around the private nine-hole course running past the compound's various full-size homes.

Every detail's been scrutinized. Every possible need met. No excuses.

Not only am I the favorite going into these Olympics, the entire US cycling team is full of odds-on contenders. My best friend and team-mate, Erin Hartwell, is looking to improve on his Olympic bronze medal in the 1-kilometer time trial. Our team pursuit squad is nailing world-record times in training. Juli Furtado is the reigning World Cup champion in cross-country mountain biking. The number-one-ranked road cyclist during the 1996 season? Lance Armstrong.

· · · · · · · · · ·

The Olympic match sprint starts with a 200-meter time trial. Only 24 competitors will make it into the tournament. The fastest qualifier will face the slowest in the first round, and so on. The better I ride in this qualifier, the easier my road to the finals.

The time trial is a flying start: two and a half laps, alone, on the track; the last 200 meters for time. I start on the back straight and ride along the top of the track's steep banking. The Atlanta velodrome is built with special composite-wood boards and my rear disc wheel hums as it rolls over the smooth panels. *Whoosh. Whoosh. Whoosh.* I cross the finish line. Two laps to go. I'm wearing a Stars-and-Stripes skinsuit designed by Pearl Izumi specifically for these games—custom tailored to reduce drag.

No excuses.

In the far turn I climb out of the saddle. I roll the handlebars in my hands. The bike sways back and forth beneath my body. I start ramping up my speed as I approach the finish line again. *Faster.* One lap to go. *Faster.* 200 meters.

Everything.

I point my bike at the apex of the track's first turn and dive down the banking. I continue to accelerate as I fly along the bottom edge of the back straight. Every pedal stroke is a focused effort. I pummel each downstroke of the crankarms with the full force of my legs, butt, and back. My upper body is braced against the bike's steel handlebars by my hulking arms. I funnel every ounce of power toward my rear wheel.

My bike is equipped with just one gear: 49 teeth on the front chainring, 14 on the rear cog. It is a fixed gear, meaning it doesn't coast. Nor does the bike have brakes. The faster I spin my legs, the faster I propel my bike. Entering the far turn my legs are a massive flesh-colored whir beneath my nearly motionless torso.

I'm traveling more than 45 miles per hour. I'm riding so fast the g-forces try to pull my bike up the banking. But I stay smooth, steering my bike low toward the bottom edge of the track. I take the fastest route to the finish.

The effort is only 10 seconds long, but it's 100 percent anaerobic. The lack of oxygen forces lactic acid to overwhelm my body. But I feel no pain. I'm fueled by an onslaught of adrenaline. My strength feels inhuman.

I'm sitting in the saddle, spinning 160 revolutions per minute.

My back is arched. My elbows are pointed out.

In my mind, I'm fighting for survival. When I sprint, I'm lifting a car from my body after a wreck. I'm fighting off a bear. I'm sprinting for my life.

I round the last turn. The finish line enters my blurry field of vision. *Fight. Fight. Fight. Fight. Fight.*

I cross the line. 10.176. Olympic record.

· · · · · · · · ·

My record lasts 15 minutes. The Australian Gary Neiwand rides 10.129 seconds, setting the new Olympic standard and qualifying first. A Canadian, Curt Harnett—the current world-record holder in the flying 200 meters and the first man to go under 10 seconds—qualifies second. He beats me by 1 millisecond (one thousandth of a second). I'm seeded third. My biggest rival, the 1992 Olympic gold medalist, Germany's Jens Fiedler, qualifies directly behind me.

I win my first- and second-round matches easily, against lesser opponents. In the quarterfinals I face Australian Darryn Hill. The winner will make it to the semifinals, which will include the last four sprinters—those who'll compete for medals. Hill is a pit bull on a bicycle. Though he stands 4 inches shorter than me, he weighs nearly the same. His stocky body is solid muscle. Away from reporters, he speaks in a stream of Aussie cuss words.

Hill is perhaps the only person in the world who can maneuver a track bike as well as me. We both grew up racing BMX (bicycle motocross), and Hill was a star in the discipline before turning to track cycling as a teenager. He rides wheelies around the velodrome apron to celebrate victories. Like me, he doesn't avoid contact on the track. He thrives on it. Give him a sliver of room at the bottom of the track and he'll dive underneath you, putting an elbow in your ribs for good measure as he passes.

Hill and I have history. I beat him in '94 for the world championship. In '95, he redeemed himself by winning the gold medal at worlds. He comes into these Games the reigning champion. When we face each other, people who understand cycling stop what they're doing to watch us compete. Racers warming up turn their attention to the action on the track. Officials, coaches, and track cycling dignitaries set their eyes upon our match.

Hill's veteran teammate, Neiwand, tells me our matches get so intense because we're so similar. "You're both lunatics," he says.

I anticipate a battle. But the pressure of the Olympics is weighing on Hill. He underperforms. I outthink him, then outmuscle him. He lacks top-end speed. In the first match I beat him from the front, holding him off by half a wheel. In the second match I come around him in the final turn and win by half a bike length.

The pit bull's been muzzled. On to the next round.

In the semifinals I meet Harnett. He's big and tall like me. As his world-record 200-meter time trial attests, he's best at max speed. Also like me. But if Hill's a pit bull, Harnett's a golden retriever. Curly blond locks flow from the back of his helmet. He's even appeared in shampoo commercials. He's subdued. Docile. Canadian.

It's late July in Georgia—the Deep South—infamous for its sweltering humidity. A 4-hour rain delay has pushed back the schedule from the cooler morning and intensified the velodrome's mid-afternoon mugginess. Riding around the banked oval feels like pedaling through a bowl of warm soup. After three rounds of sprinting in this heat, Harnett's hurting. But I'm just hitting my stride.

The crowd is electric. I'm charged. I ride Harnett up and down the track. He's pinned against the ropes. I win the draw heading into the first sprint, meaning I'll assume the lead on the first lap. Just the way I like it. Harnett sits a few lengths off my rear wheel and tails me as I soft-pedal around the track. I keep one eye in front of me, one eye in back.

If he wants the front, he'll have to earn it. But he waits way too long. I see him coming and start to ramp up my speed. By the time we hit the final 200 meters, I'm in full gallop. He can't get past me. I beat him by half a bike length.

Harnett leads the second sprint off the start line. The first sprint was long. Grueling. He's tired. His reflexes are slow. I ride high on the banking behind him, as if I'm going to pass on his outside. This forces Harnett to ride high too. He's trying to block me, to nail me against track's top rail. He's looking over his right shoulder, looking forward. Right shoulder. Forward.

With a lap to go he looks over his right shoulder, but I'm not there anymore. I make a hard left and drop off the top of the track underneath Harnett. The crowd explodes. I'm gone. Sprinting all-out. He's broken. I win easily by two bike lengths.

Typically in a match-sprint tournament, the semifinal and finals take place on the same day. But at the Atlanta Olympics, because of TV, the finals are the next day. It's the only race I've ever done with a format like this. The crowd is rabid. I'm riding great. The momentum is on my side. I want to race now. But I know going into the race with Harnett, I'll have to wait.

I go back to the compound. It's still not over. Tomorrow I race for gold.

· · · · · · · ·

It's 1976 and I'm 5 years old. I sit next to my mom in front of the TV and watch the Montreal Olympics. Nadia Comaneci scores a perfect 10 on the uneven bars. Bruce Jenner wins gold in the decathlon. A teenager named Greg Louganis takes silver in diving on the 10-meter platform. I'm enthralled with the pageantry of the Olympics and intensity of the competition. I'm only 5 and the Olympic dream is becoming my dream, already.

An athlete on the TV bends forward as the gold medal is draped around his neck. The national anthem plays. I jump up on the coffee table and raise my arms.

"I'm going to win the Olympics someday," I shout.

Cute, my mom thinks.

· · · · · · · ·

More rain crashes down on Stone Mountain the Sunday morning of the match-sprint finals. It peels down the rock's smooth face in thick sheets. The track is too slick to race on. So we wait. It's a long wait. The kind of wait that tests athletes' nerves and makes them wonder if today really is *their* day. This kind of wait cracks a lot of athletes. I see it all the time. I see it in athletes' eyes. I can tell who's going to crack just by looking at them. Two days before the event, they're riding world-record pace. Then they tank.

Some athletes say the Olympics are just like any other event. I'm going to approach the Games just as I would any other race, they say. They try to take the pressure off by denying that it exists. I do the opposite. The Olympics are not just another event. This is the biggest sporting event in the world. And you better bring your best, because everyone else is bringing theirs.

I'm not nervous, even as the rain pelts the putting green outside our rental house, and we keep waiting. I pride myself on being unflinching. I'm like Stone Mountain. Control what you can control, I tell myself. I thrive on the pressure. I feed off it. The closer the race gets, the more excited I become. I can't wait to get it on.

On the TV there's nothing but news about the explosion that occurred at 1:30 a.m. on Saturday in Olympic Park. A woman died. A hundred more people suffered horrendous shrapnel wounds from a crudely made pipe bomb. I'm pictured in *Sports Illustrated* observing a moment of silence before Saturday's semi- and quarterfinals.

"It's a shame and my heart's out to everybody," I tell Gary Blockus from the *Morning Call*, my hometown paper. "But I'm here to win a medal at the Olympic Games and nobody's going to stop me." Control what you can control.

Today is the last day of track cycling at the Olympics. And so far, the USA Cycling team has underperformed, horribly. The only medal came from Erin Hartwell, Erv, the guy I've roomed with on the national team since I was 18. Erv and I are peas in a pod. Best buds. We bring the same tenacity to training and racing. He was born in Philadelphia and raised in Indiana. Erv shares my blue-collar work ethic. He's also dreamed about the Olympics since he was kid. Neither of us believe we're capable of losing.

Erv is my leadoff hitter. He sets the bar, and I try to clear it. On Wednesday he rips the 1-kilometer time trial on his Superbike and bests his previous Olympic performance by a podium spot. He brings a silver medal back to our house. He's ecstatic. I'm pumped. Now go get the gold, he tells me. I'm USA Cycling's last opportunity to justify Project '96—hundreds of thousands of dollars' worth of pressure.

Finally, the track dries. Time to race. I'm ready. I face the German, Jens Fiedler. He's the defending Olympic champion, a vestige of the East German sprinting machine. These athletes didn't choose sprinting, they were chosen. Fiedler studied under Lutz Hesslich, the most feared match sprinter ever. Hesslich won the 1980 Olympics, skipped '84 because of the boycott, then came back and won again in '88. The Germans are methodical and precise. They expose their opponents, then mercilessly dissect them.

Fiedler's sprinting style is absent of holes. He's bulletproof tactically and among the quickest in the world. Give him a sliver of space and he's gone. I'm faster than him at top speed. The problem is, he knows it. The tactic is out on me. He will race me from the front. He knows if I have the front, he can't come around me.

USA Cycling sprint coach Andrzej Bek holds me on the start line. Andrzej's from Poland and won his own bronze medal on the tandem at the 1972 Olympics. He's been with me since I won worlds in '94. He brings an Eastern European mentality to competition. He knows how tough Fiedler is, but for some reason, tells the press that I've intimidated Fiedler recently. We'll find out. He doesn't look scared.

No excuses, says Andrzej.

My personal coach, Gil Hatton, stands at the track's apron. He wants to hold me on the start line, I can tell. Gil's trained me since I first set foot on a velodrome as a scrawny 15-year-old. Over the years he's morphed from my mentor to my training partner to my closest confidant. Every battle we've fought together over the last decade culminates in this moment. I'll need every trick he taught me to win this race.

I reach down and yank on the leather straps that hold my feet into the pedals. Two straps on each foot, pulled tight like nooses. If my foot comes out of the pedal, I'm done. If I crash, I'll crash with my bike, machine and man tumbling across the track together. I say a prayer, as I do before every race, not to crash. I pray my competitor and I will stay safe. I'm not especially religious, but if there's a time to believe in God, this is it.

Andrzej leans into my ear. His voice is the deepest I've ever heard, and it's thickened by his Polish accent. "You must take the front," he says. *Fuck, Andrzej*, I think, *I know*.

I look over at Fiedler on my inside, closer to the apron. He's wearing a black-and-white skinsuit with swatches of orange and yellow German stripes. His helmet is an aerodynamic round, white cap that makes him look like a water polo player. He sits atop a black carbon-fiber bike with thick, bladed tubes. His body is a specimen: 6 feet tall, 200 pounds, not an ounce of fat on him.

I prayed we won't get hurt, but I want to kill him. I want to rip his fucking throat out. I want to win this race, and I want to make his death quick, decisive.

Fiedler takes a deep breath and stares straight ahead. He shoots the air out of his narrow nose in three quick bursts. Then he puts on his dark sunglasses. It's time to race. The official looks at Fiedler, he nods. The official looks at me. I nod. Fiedler's won the prerace draw. He assumes the lead.

· · · · · · · · ·

Fiedler does exactly as I suspect. He's riding defensively, guarding the front. He doesn't want me to pass. And because he's required to lead the first lap, it makes his job a lot easier. He eyes me as I stalk him from a few bike lengths back. As we round the backstretch, I start to wind up my sprint.

I make a charge at him. One quick burst to pass him and claim the front, then guard the position until I'm ready to sprint for the line. But Fiedler sees me coming. He opens up, and because he's so goddamn quick, it takes him no time to match my speed. I draw even with him through the fourth turn. We're shoulder to shoulder, elbow to elbow. I'm leaning into him as we enter the home straight. But Fiedler won't back down, even though I outweigh him by 25 pounds. He keeps me high on the track's banking, making me ride a longer distance to get around him. He's not intimidated at all.

I back down. We've traded jabs, and Fiedler has landed one on my chin. I won't outmuscle him. So I try to trick him, just like Harnett. I'll fake that I'm coming over the top and try to drop underneath, anything to get back to the front. But he's bulletproof tactically. He's more experienced than me and he learned from one of the best, ever. He positions perfectly. There's no room for me to drop underneath him or come over the top.

If I'm going to see the front of this race it will be a few feet before the finish line. I must time my sprint perfectly, using Fiedler's draft to build my speed and pass him just before the line. One lap to go. Fiedler starts winding up his sprint. By the middle of the first turn he's flying, and I'm planted right behind him, aiming for his right hip.

We hit the back straight. Fiedler accelerates. He's going faster, faster, all the way to the finish line 200 meters away. But I'm gaining, narrowing the gap to his rear wheel. I'm still in the draft, but the draft diminishes as I move to his right and prepare to pass. The air breaks over the front of his body like the wake coming off a boat. Behind him it's placid and smooth. Sprinting is effortless. But to Fiedler's right, the turbulence of the air starts to hit me. I'm in the choppy surf, and I must pedal twice as hard.

So I do. We're in the final turn and he can feel me coming, bringing more speed. I'm going to whip past him as we drop out of the last turn onto the homestretch. But Fiedler rides higher on the track than a sprinter normally would. Normally the front rider takes the quickest route to the finish, low on the track, which also leaves no space for an opponent to sneak underneath them. But he stays above the red line denoting the sprinter's lane.

Fiedler knows track-racing rules dictate that once a rider establishes a low position, below the red line, he can't leave. He's the German tactician. If he's in the sprinter's lane, he can't legally move up on the track

to block me from passing. He can't hook me without risking disqualification. A hook is a violent whip of the bike up the boards, which breaks
your competitor's momentum. It forces him to back off the pressure on
the pedals just for a moment, and takes away the advantage gained from
sprinting in your draft. To the casual spectator, a properly thrown hook
looks like an unintentional loss of control. But believe me, at this level,
no hook is unintentional.

We race into the final turn. My front wheel draws even with
Fiedler's rear wheel. Then it comes: He flicks his bike just a foot to the
right, trying to beat me back. We're going 45 miles per hour, and
Fiedler's swerving at me. But I anticipate his hook. I adjust, and by the
middle of the turn I'm at his hip. I'm reaching my max speed as we
sweep into the finishing straight. I'm flying up on Fiedler, but it might
be too late. Fifty meters to the line, and every 10 meters I make up a
foot. I'm at his hip, his shoulder, still gaining, there's the line. The first
front wheel across the tape wins. We lunge, throwing our bikes in front
of us with our arms outstretched and our heads down.

We're mirror images of each other. We cross the line and I sail in
front of Fiedler.

Photo finish.

. . . .

The officials go to the tape. The camera, shooting 10,000 frames per
second, decides my fate. But I don't need a camera to know I crossed the
line first. Every racer knows whether they won or lost, no matter how
close the finish. It's instinctual. I'm my own camera. Even NASCAR
drivers traveling 200 miles per hour can tell if he won or lost by an inch.
But my victory is in the hands of the officials.

After 20 minutes, they come back with an answer. I lost. I know I
won, but they prove me wrong. An official says Fiedler beat me by a
centimeter. By one thousandth of a second.

I'm deflated, down one ride to the reigning Olympic champ. I must take the next two sprints to win gold. The sky is dreary and dark. The crowd is quiet, the energy and excitement from the day before gone. We think about protesting the result. But what are we going to show them that they haven't already seen?

Screw it, I say. Let's go kick Fiedler's ass, right now—twice in a row.

We line up. I'm on the inside now, leading out the first lap, unless Fiedler wants to pass me, which he will. I reach down and tighten my straps. "You must control the front," says the deepest voice I've ever heard. *Fuck, Andrzej. I know!*

The officials look at me, I nod. They look at Fiedler, he nods. Go. Andrzej pushes me. Fiedler's coach pushes him, only much harder. He's half a wheel in front of me right off the line. He takes three hard pedal strokes and claims the front. *Fuck!*

Same game. I charge Fiedler. He holds me off. I try to dive underneath him. He protects the inside of the track. He keeps me at bay until he's ready to start his sprint. He won't let me reach my max speed. He knows he'll lose. One lap to go. Fiedler's weaving all over the track as I charge toward his rear wheel. He's above the sprinter's lane, below the sprinter's lane. Never flagrant enough to draw the ire of the officials, just enough to keep me at bay. I'd do the same thing, if I had the front.

We round the last corner, and again I'm gaining ground on him. I'm the faster rider. I reach his hip, his shoulder, there's the line. Fiedler beats me by half a wheel.

He wins the gold medal. I lose.

· · · · · · · · ·

It's 5 days before the Games and I'm hitting golf balls with Andrzej, Gil, and Erv. I hit a ball into one of the little ponds dotting the course. I reach toward the pond to get the ball, and spot a water moccasin, curled up right next to my hand. It's looking back at me. I dare you, it's saying.

Oh shit. I don't panic. I slowly pull my hand away from the pond. I leave the golf ball right there. I think, *some things happen for a reason.*

. . . .

As we let the gears spin out on our bikes, I ride next to Fiedler. I shake his hand. I rub his round, white helmet. He pumps his fist in the air, triumphantly. It was a fair fight, a good match. I lost to a worthy competitor, one of the greatest Olympic track cyclists of all time. I ride over to my family sitting in the front row of the bleachers.

I haven't touched them in a month. I isolate myself during the Games, and they know to give me space when I'm competing. We talk once per day on the phone. That's it. Now I wonder if that isolation was worth it. I love my family. I kiss Christi, my fiancée, and squeeze Tyler, my 17-month-old son. My mom and dad, separated since I was in middle school, and my siblings congratulate me. My younger brother, Jay, my closest ally throughout childhood, slaps me on the back.

What do you say to someone who just lost gold? They tell me what they think I'll want to hear. Boy, that first race was close. We think you won it, too, they say. My mom is in a wheelchair. She broke her leg in the spring, and suffered a complication from a blood clot during the competition. Of course, she made the family promise not to tell me what happened. She's hoarse from screaming during the races. (Even though she refuses to watch anything but the last lap, for fear I'll crash.) "We'll get him in 4 years! The year 2000!" she tells reporters.

"All in all, I'm extremely happy," I tell the press. "We accomplished the goal of winning an Olympic medal." I say all the right things. I give the quotes people expect. I say what you expect of an Olympian, a world-class athlete. I speak the words of someone with endorsement dollars on the line. Part of me even believes what I'm saying.

I put on my Olympic podium tracksuit, a special uniform every athlete is given, but only those who participate in a medal ceremony get to wear. I stand atop the medal podium. I raise my arms for the obligatory photo ops. All the while a quiet rage starts building inside me. My mind absorbs what my body just experienced. It makes me mad. I'm the fastest rider in the world, and I lost on my home soil, in front of my family and my friends. I waited my entire life for this moment, and I let it slip through my hands. I lost because I made a tactical mistake. The German national anthem plays, and I nearly snap. I want to punch Fiedler's lights out. I harness every ounce of mental restraint to keep from physically tackling Fiedler off the top step.

I walk back to the little cubicle, called the cabin, each team gets on the infield of the track. Andrzej and Gil and my masseuse, Eddie Balcerzak, are there, packing. They're happy. We got a medal. We should go home, clean up, celebrate. Right?

I see my bike. Silver. I hate silver. I let everyone down. I let down my coaches, my family, my country.

Damn. Damn. Damn. Fuck! I think. I toss the medal onto a table as if it's a bag of nickels. "I didn't come here for this fucking color," I say. Andrzej, Gil, and Eddie stare at me blankly. What do you say? *Shit,* they think.

"We start training for Sydney tomorrow," I growl.

2
MY KIND OF SPORT

I REACH down and pick up another round river stone from the edge of our house's aboveground pool. I cock my arm back, aim, and release the stone like an outfielder throwing to home. It soars from our side yard, across the street, and hits the neighbor's roof—*thwack!* The rock rolls off the roof onto the lawn. My little brother, Jay, smirks. He's 13 years old, 1 year younger than me, and my partner in hell-raising. He can beat that. He launches a rock that hits the garage door square on the top panel. *Thwack!* I can beat that. *Thwack!*

Inside the neighbor's house, Mike Walter, 26 years old, sits in his wheelchair. He's paralyzed from the neck down. He was riding his bike on a nearby road, when a drunk driver hit him from behind. At the time of the accident, Mike was one of the top young cyclists in the United States, 18 years old and headed to the junior world championships, to be held at the track right here in Trexlertown. Now he'll never pedal a bike again.

His dad, Heinz, the manager of the Panasonic Shimano professional cycling team, is out shopping. Mike is at home with his friend Ian Jackson, a racer from Australia. Mike can't be at home alone. They hear the rocks slamming against the garage door. Ian goes outside to see what the hell is going on. He spots Jay and me.

We run inside and hide.

We're not looking for trouble. We're just bored. There's not a single other kid our age in the neighborhood—just a bunch of half-built houses

and big mounds of dirt. We race our BMX bikes up and down the dirt
mounds. We jump in the pool. Then, for some reason, we start throwing
rocks. We know it's wrong. We're just bored.

Jay and I peek out the window from behind the blinds. Heinz's big
silver van creeps down the street and pulls into the driveway. The side
of the van is decorated with a bike rider and racing stripes. The riders'
names are hand painted on the side. Heinz climbs out. He sees the
rocks. They're scattered all over his perfectly trimmed lawn. He picks
them up. He counts more than 30 stones. He puts them in a card-
board box. He sees the dents in his garage door, shakes his head, and
walks inside.

Moments later, here Heinz comes, strutting across the street, card-
board box in hand. Heinz immigrated to New York from Germany as a
kid. He's part German, part New Yorker, a ferocious combination.
We're scared to death of him. He always has his eye on us. He frequently casts us glares from across the street. It makes our knees weak.

Thump, thump, thump!

He's knocking on the door. Answer it, Jay says, *Crap.* I open the
door.

"We didn't do it!" I say.

"Let me tell you something," Heinz says. "Anybody throws any
more stones at my house, I break your arm off!"

He drops the stones right there at the entrance to our house. Then
he leaves.

· · · · · · · · ·

An hour later my mom, Gail, comes home. Round two. She sees the
box of rocks. "What the hell is this?" she asks. Here we go, back across
the street. She's got a handful of Jay's hair in one hand, my hair in the
other. I'm a big kid, tall and rangy, but I don't mess with my mom
when she's pissed.

Heinz opens the door.

"My kids have something to tell you," my mom says.

"I'm sorry," Jay says.

"I'm sorry," I say.

We're looking at Heinz's feet. Heinz thinks for a second.

"Come downstairs with me," he finally says. He takes us into his basement, where he keeps all the team's bikes and equipment. They're custom painted, identically. Each bike is adorned with bleach white handlebar tape. Everything white, everything gleaming. It's the Heinz treatment. The chrome parts shine under the fluorescent lamps. Heinz explains to us how the racing bikes work. Jay and I stare at the bikes, awestruck.

Heinz knows Jay and I will like the bikes. He and Mike have watched us ripping around the neighborhood, up and down the dirt mounds, and they're impressed. "Those kids, they're fearless," Mike tells his dad.

"Why don't you do something productive, instead of just throwing stones?" Heinz says to me. "Throwing stones doesn't get you nowhere."

"Look, there's a program for kids your age at the velodrome," Heinz says. He knows my dad is Pennsylvania Dutch, as cheap as they come, and would never buy me a track bike. "It's free, sponsored by Air Products," Heinz tells me.

"They'll even let you borrow a bike," he says.

Out of guilt, more than anything, I say okay.

"Okay, I'll give it a shot. I'll try out the velodrome," I say.

· · · · · · · · ·

In the afternoons, when my mom is at work, Jay and I watch *Happy Days. Who the hell are these people?* we wonder. I know my mom and dad love me and all the rest of their children intensely, but in no way is my upbringing ideal.

My family is directly descended from the German immigrants enticed to settle in America by William Penn, the namesake of Pennsylvania. Prior to the Revolutionary War, tens of thousands of Germans immigrated to Pennsylvania, seeking religious freedom and lush farmland. In the fertile plains and rolling hills of the Lehigh Valley, about 60 miles north of Philadelphia, these immigrants adopted a farming lifestyle similar to the one they had led in their homeland.

(Though, not all of the Germans came to Pennsylvania as farmers. A band of feared mercenaries, the Hessians, fought alongside the British redcoats during the Revolutionary War.).

In the Lehigh Valley, these German immigrants are now known as the Pennsylvania Dutch (or simply, PA Dutch). "Dutch" is related to *Deutsch*, the German word for "German." The PA Dutch here even speak their own dialect of the German language. I listen to my dad and my grandparents speak PA Dutch growing up. I never learn the unique idiom myself, other than the correct German pronounciation of our family's last name, Note-Stine.

The PA Dutch take pride in their blue-collar work ethic and propensity for physical labor. They eschew a lavish lifestyle (to the point of obsessive stinginess) and invest in property before all else. Family comes first and foremost for the PA Dutch. Cultural delicacies include the fluffy, molasses-filled shoofly pie; stuffed pig stomach; and liver and onions. Yum.

My dad's PA Dutch stinginess sometimes forces my family to live below our means. My first bike is a used girl's bike because my dad doesn't see the need for something newer and sex appropriate. I miss out on school field trips because the meager cost is deemed frivolous. Toughness is a prized trait, often instilled in us at the expense of affection. My family considers privacy sacred—even when it comes to our own emotions. I'm taught to never cry. Tears are for the weak, I'm told.

My dad wooed my mom when he was only 21, ingratiating himself to her parents by speaking their PA Dutch dialect. He grew up in the car business, starting out as a semi driver for his dad, and later inheriting the Nothstein trucking company, along with his brother. They manage a fleet of nearly 50 trucks and own more state-granted rights to haul limestone than any other trucking company in Pennsylvania. During my childhood he also owns a Ford and a Dodge dealership and acquires a number of local houses.

My dad works hard and ends nearly every day with a stop at the bar before coming home. Just a couple of drinks with the guys, he says. But too often, he's home late, reeking of booze. My mom used to yell at him, but she's done yelling now. Now she waits by the front door, tears welling in her eyes.

Many nights Dad doesn't come home at all. Mom knows booze isn't Dad's only vice. He charmed her once, too. So Mom loads me into the car and we go looking for Dad, driving around town to his known haunts. Eventually though, Mom stops looking.

My dad gets a letter in the mail from my mom's lawyer. My mom is seeking a divorce, and it's best if he moves out. Though he doesn't admit to any transgressions, and never will, my dad agrees to leave the home and custody of the kids to my mom. He moves to his hunting cabin on Christman Lake, 20 miles away.

My gregarious older sisters, Waynette and Carlene, born a decade ahead of Jay and me, help my mom raise me. In my dad's absence, our family's oldest child, Tim, is part big brother, part father figure. He coaches Jay's and my Little League teams.

Though I never feel unloved or neglected, the fact my parents aren't always around, that my home life isn't like the other kids', often makes me angry. Really angry.

· · · · · · · · ·

I know of the velodrome, but I don't actually know anything about the velodrome. My family's Dodge dealership backs up to the parkland the velodrome sits on. Every Friday night during the racing season, I see the flags waving and the lights beaming high above the track. I can hear the roar of the crowd and the excited voice of the announcer crackling over the PA system, calling out the names of riders from far away countries such as Switzerland, Australia, and Germany.

Nothing could seem more out of place in the farmland surrounding Trexlertown than a velodrome. Locals dub the complex the crater in the cornfield. But week after week, the community programs and pro racing at the velodrome extend the reach of track cycling to a completely new demographic, which includes me.

I'm told the track exists because of Robert "Bob" Rodale, chairman and CEO of Rodale Press Inc. Rodale was an Olympic skeet shooter. He even represented the United States at the 1968 Games in Mexico City. It was during his international competitions that Rodale first saw track cycling and became captivated by the sport.

Though he never raced, Rodale had a fondness for bicycles. He frequently took long rides in the countryside to clear his mind (and to satisfy his other passion, discovering and collecting old Volkswagens). After the Olympics, he envisioned a velodrome in the Lehigh Valley that would provide a recreational and competitive outlet. So, in 1974, he donated 25 acres of farmland to the county and oversaw the construction of an unusual new park, which would contain the nation's premier bicycle-racing track.

As word of the new velodrome spread, a handful of ardent track racers from the East Coast arrived in the Lehigh Valley. Dave Chauner and Jack Simes, a pair of Olympic cyclists, were hired as the new velodrome's directors. Chauner and Simes knew how to put on a show. They hired an organ player to accompany the Friday night pro races and drew top international talent to competitions. Even Eddy Merckx, the greatest cyclist who ever lived, appeared at the track in 1978.

The track, and the small town surrounding it, became known simply as T-Town.

Families even relocated to the Lehigh Valley because of the new velo-drome. That's how Heinz and his son Mike, who lived in New York City and raced at the ragged Kissena velodrome, ended up in Trexlertown. Heinz had heard about the track and was anxiously awaiting its comple-tion. Then, one night, he had an inkling that the velodrome was done. "Load up the car," he told Mike. "We're going to ride the new track."

When Heinz arrived at T-Town, only Bob Rodale was there, check-ing in on the progress of the constructed, but not yet fully finished, velodrome. Mike and Heinz rolled their bikes up to the edge of the site, where Rodale stopped them. "I'm sorry, you can't ride the track yet," he said in a diplomatic, but firm voice.

Heinz, who had no clue that the man speaking to him was respon-sible for the track's existence, replied in his guttural German accent, "Now you look here! My son and I drove all the way from New York to ride this track and I'll be damned if anyone stops us."

With that, Heinz took Rodale's shoulder, steered him out of the way, and rode onto the track. Rodale, taken aback both by Heinz's abra-siveness and his passion, didn't intervene. After moving to Trexlertown, Heinz Walter and the Rodale family became close friends. The Rodales even briefly housed Mike's mother after his tragic accident so she could be near the hospital where he was being treated.

· · · · · · · · ·

Growing up, I'm taken by all things competitive. During my parents separation, I temporarily live at my grandmother's house in Allentown. One day I'm playing basketball by myself on a court near the rougher part of town when a group of local kids surround me. They intimidate me and take my ball. I go home and tell my grandma what happened. Go get it back, she says.

The next day I show up at the court and the kids are playing with my ball. I whip their butts. I get my ball back. The next day, and the day after, I show up again. I don't want to play basketball. I just want to fight. I learn that I like fighting. I'm a fighter. (Maybe I have a little Hessian in me.)

Jay and I pummel each other so badly and regularly that my mom asks the family doctor, "Is this normal?" She's concerned. But my fighting spirit makes me good at sports. I love sports. Baseball: I rip the bat as if I'm trying to decapitate someone. Football: I can run full speed, right into this kid with two happily married parents at home? Yes, please. Wrestling: I pin my opponents with such tenacity that the coaches tell my mom I can't come back. He's hurting the other children, they say.

When I show up to the velodrome for the first day of practice, as part of the Air Products developmental program—wearing cut-off jean shorts and riding my BMX bike—I'm not looking for friends or a fun time. I'm looking to beat the shit out of some people.

I like racing more than any ball sport. Track cycling requires speed and tenacity, traits I possess. But best of all, I no longer must depend on teammates to win. If I perform, the rewards follow.

One Friday night, Jay and I watch the pros race from underneath the bleachers on the back straight. We know the racers dish out their most vitriolic barbs and semi-legal tactics on the side of the track opposite where most of the spectators sit. On this evening, Mark Whitehead, nicknamed the Outlaw, a pro racer for the team Heinz manages, is dominating the pack with his superior fitness and bike handling—as well as through sheer intimidation. He's whipping the crowd into a roaring frenzy.

As the riders round the second turn of the track, Whitehead is jostling for position with Pat McDonough, an Air Products coach and an Olympic medalist. As the pack sweeps past us, Whitehead knocks Pat's wheels out from under him, sending him flying across the track and down onto the blacktop that rings the bottom of the banking. Pat's wearing pearl white patent leather shoes that leave two parallel stripes as they slide across the asphalt—like a pair of thick chalk lines scrawled across a blackboard.

Speed. Aggression. Showmanship. This is my kind of sport, I decide.

· · · · · · · · · ·

Though I've never ridden on a velodrome before, I'm no rookie bike racer. My two brothers and I grew up riding motocross, until my older brother, Tim, crashed and shattered his ankle in a race. My dad decided no more motorcycles, but offered to let me race either go-Karts or BMX. I chose BMX, figuring it more closely resembled motocross, and started tearing up dirt tracks across the Lehigh Valley. With my BMX experience, I quickly graduate from the beginner Air Products classes into the more advanced program.

A pro named Gil Hatton (or, Gibby, to most of the racing community) is assigned as my coach. All the kids know about Gil. He's one of the best sprinters in the world, and a crowd favorite at the Friday night pro races. We both admire and fear him.

He's nicknamed the Bear, and rightly so. Gil's barrel chest is supported by a pair of short, thick legs. His helmet does little to contain his mop of curly black hair. A thick mustache adorns his upper lip. He's notorious for his volatility, which draws me to him. I know Gil's always up for a good fight.

Gil's just as much a part of the velodrome's history as anyone in T-Town. He grew up in Southern California and started racing on a small track in Encino. Soon, he was beating up on every kid in the state, then the country, and then the world. In 1974 he won the junior world championships and was heralded as America's next Olympic medal hope.

But Gil started running with the wrong crowd after high school and forsook any Olympic aspirations. He'd been to T-Town before and knew that a bike racer could make a living riding the track there—that local girls fawned over the top riders and celebratory beers flowed freely at local pubs for the victors on Friday nights.

One evening in 1980, Gil was hanging out beside a friend's pool near LA, partying, when he decided to come east. "Pack up your shit," he told Pat McDonough, who was a few years younger than Gil at the time and owned the car they would drive to T-Town. "We're leaving tonight."

Gil knew that in order to salvage his cycling career he needed to leave California. "I'm going, and I'm never coming back," he told his dad, who'd driven him all over the country, to all those junior races. He loved his dad more than anyone.

Gil and Pat's trip east would become T-Town lore. Adamant that Gil was too intoxicated to drive, Pat took the wheel and pointed his Plymouth Champ toward the desert. The sun was just cresting on the horizon when Gil was jolted awake. Pat had fallen asleep at the wheel, and the car rolled off the side of the road, somersaulting several times before landing in the sandy brush. Dirt covered everything inside and outside the vehicle.

They'd only made it 140 miles from LA. Gil groggily looked over at Pat, who had blood matted in his dusty hair. After realizing neither of them was dead, he said, "I'm going to fucking kill you!" Their bikes were trashed, and the car was barely drivable, but Gil remained set on getting out of California. He kicked out the shattered front window, got the car towed back up onto I-40, tied a bandana around his mouth and nose to keep out the bugs, and continued the trip eastward.

Days later, the pair drew the eyes of every racer at the T-Town velodrome when they pulled into the gravel parking lot. The car's frame was bent, and though the wheels tracked a semi-straight line, the crumpled vehicle looked as if it was constantly making a right turn. Only one set of bike wheels survived the crash, so Gil and Pat flipped a coin every

Friday night to see who got to race. Gil earned enough in prize money to buy new parts, and eventually he became the Bear, one of T-Town's top sprinters.

Now, he's my coach.

. . . .

During practice one day Gil overhears me bragging to the other kids. He's sick of me showing off during practice and cutting up while we're working out.

"Hey smart ass," Gil shouts at me. "Why don't you see how you fare against me, then." He proposes a 3-kilometer pursuit. I cockily accept. Gil starts on the home straight. I line up on the opposite side of the track. The first cyclist to ride nine laps and cross his own finish line, wins.

I'm a freshman in high school and as awkward-looking as they come: 6 feet tall and 160 pounds, with a wispy mullet. Gil's 31 and is still morphing from a youthful punk himself into a cagey vet.

We start.

I put my head down and pedal as hard as I can. I'm too new to know how to pace myself. I just go all-out. Three laps in, I look across the track. We're even. But Gil knows exactly how to gauge his effort. Six laps in and he's pulling away. I'm wobbling. Falling apart. My long arms and legs shoot out in every direction. We approach the finish; Gil cruises across the line a couple of seconds in front of me. He's breathing through his nose.

"I'll give you 10 minutes, then you're doing a 200-meter sprint," Gil says.

I scowl at Gil, but inside I'm ecstatic. The battle continues.

I'm too young to know I shouldn't be able to sprint after an all-out pursuit effort. I take a flying start for the 200, dropping off the top of the track as Gil showed us, gaining speed, hugging the apron. I cross the finish and Gil thumbs his stopwatch: 11.7 seconds. Just a half second off the junior track record, set by a Soviet rider when the junior world championships were here in T-Town. Holy shit, Gil thinks, this kid is good.

"Get back over there with the other kids," he growls at me.

· · · · · · · · ·

I love racing, but I'm just 15 and other sports still interest me, too. I do all the community programs, but I also go months without riding. Luckily, Heinz and Mike are keeping tabs on me. Mike's mom, Inga, rolls him out onto their driveway in the afternoons so he can get some sun. I see him on my way home from training rides, and I stop to talk.

I tell Mike that I'm getting dropped from the Derby, T-Town's Sunday morning hammerfest; that my track stand still needs work; and that I even sometimes struggle to get my foot in the toe straps of my pedal at the start of road races. Mike offers me encouragement, sharing some of the same tips he learned as one of the country's top junior racers. Now that I race, Heinz no longer glares at me as he used to. But I still approach him gingerly. I know he's tougher on cyclists than anyone else. When one of the racers he manages does poorly, he marks over his name on the side of the team van with black tape until the rider eventually redeems himself.

Mike must give Heinz updates on my progress, because before the 1987 racing season, Heinz puts in a good word with USA Cycling, the sport's national federation, the Feds. I'm invited to the US Olympic Training Center in Colorado Springs, a development camp for future Olympians.

It's my first trip west and the first time I board an airplane. As we descend into the Denver airport, the snow-capped Rocky Mountains seem monstrous compared to the Appalachian hills. This sport can take me places, I realize.

In Colorado, I'm thrown in with the best kids from across the country. The national team coach, Jiri Mainus, a champion bike racer from the Czech Republic wakes us up at 6 a.m. each day, lines us up and marches us to the cafeteria, making us perform calisthenics along the way. We swing our gangly limbs in unison, performing lunges along a snowy walkway en route to our breakfast.

After we eat, we lift weights and then spend the afternoons riding outside in subfreezing, mid-December temperatures. In the evenings, we stuff our exhausted bodies with food from the training center's corporate sponsors—including an unending supply of Mars bars. Occasionally, actual Olympians come and chat with us, handing down training and racing advice from the very top of the sport.

Train. Eat. Dream about the Olympics. Repeat.

I can live this life, I think.

· · · · · · · · ·

In the summer of 1987 the junior national championships come to Trexlertown, and Gil gets me ready. Ever since our showdown Gil lets me tag along with him. I go where he goes. We lift weights together and log miles on the narrow country roads winding through the Valley. On our rides, Gil talks to me about track racing, nonstop.

Gil comes from one of the sport's storied bloodlines, and the knowledge he passes down to me dates back to the origins of bike racing. He started racing at just 10 years old at the Encino velodrome. He tutored under Jack Disney, a three-time Olympian who dominated track cycling in the United States throughout the 1950s and '60s.

Gil tells me all about the history of the sport, about track cycling's golden era. From the turn of the 20th century through the start of World War I, track cycling was one of America's most popular sports, he says. Dozens of velodromes dotted the East Coast.

Tracks like the one at Manhattan's Madison Square Garden drew tens of thousands of spectators and offered huge sums in prize money. America's best bike racers earned double the salary of the nation's top baseball players.

Eventually though, mismanagement, the World Wars, the Great Depression, and rise of automotive racing combined to nearly wipe out track racing in the United States as a popular spectator sport. By the middle of the 20th century, track racing was all but forgotten. Just a handful of velodromes remain around the country today.

Now, most kids opt to race road bikes. They idolize Greg LeMond, who recently won his second consecutive Tour de France. But Gil teaches me to revere riders like Marshall "Major" Taylor, an African American racer from Indianapolis who broke through the color barrier en route to winning the world championship in 1899, and Frank Kramer, the last American to win a match-sprint world championship in 1912.

Over the 20th century, road racing changed dramatically. Derailleur and gear shifting advancements allowed racers to take on the high mountains, and completely changed the sport's tactics and training methods.

In contrast, track racing remained almost entirely unchanged. A track bike lacks brakes, gears, and a freewheel. The velodromes from a hundred years ago had the same banked ovals as the one here in Trexlertown. The training techniques and tactics Gil shows me were passed to him from the champion before Disney, and the champion before that, dating all the way back to the deities that ruled track racing's golden era.

Under Disney, a stoic professor of the sport, Gil mastered the fundamentals of track racing. He shows me everything: how the wind breaks over an opponent's body like a V, how the closer you get to the tip of the V, the harder it becomes to get around. He tells me to pounce when I pass. Three pedal strokes and you're beside your opponent. Bam. Bam. Bam. Three more pedal strokes and you're around him.

Gil talks to me as his own boisterous Pop Warner football coach talked to him, growling and spitting and waving his arms to get me psyched up. "It's time for payback," he booms. "Not just payback against your opponent, it's time to pay yourself back for the hard work you put in!" He calls it his Lombardi.

I've always responded to this kind of motivation. Before my own ball games my older brother, Tim, would blare AC/DC. He'd get in my ear, talking to me the whole car ride to the field. "Get in there and kick some ass," Tim would tell me. "Play as hard as you can the entire game."

Gil talks just like Tim, only louder. His speeches make the peach fuzz on my arms prick up. When I hit the track, I'm ready to kick some ass.

· · · · · · · · ·

Nationals arrive in T-Town. I face off against a couple of young guns from the East Coast with years of experience on me, Jonas Carney and George Hincapie. Jonas is from New Jersey, and his older brother, Jamie, is already a national junior champion on the track. George hails from Long Island and regularly schools senior riders at the Kissena velodrome in Queens. I'm fit and tenacious, but I'm still learning. Gil stands at the edge of the track. When he yells, I jump out of the saddle and give it hell.

Nationals for the 15 to 16 age group is an omnium format. We do a bunch of different races, and the best overall finisher wins the national title. I'm doing well, really well, never placing outside of the top three in any event. But in one of the races, I get too close to another rider and rip a bunch of spokes out of my front wheel. I don't get any points in the race, and it costs me the overall title. Jonas wins. I'm second. George is third. A local rival of mine, J. D. Moffitt, is also in the top five.

We stand on the podium and an official puts a Stars-and-Stripes jersey over Jonas's shoulders. They drape a silver medal over my neck. I look to my left, at Jonas and his new Stars-and-Stripes jersey. He's beaming. I look at my own medal. I'm 16, and I already hate silver.

· · · · · · · · · ·

I should have won. I'm good at football and I'm good at baseball, but I'm not the top player in the country.

Fall comes. Football practice starts, and I don't go.

"Mom," I say. "I'm not going to play other sports. I'm just going to race bikes."

My mom looks me up and down. "I don't think that's a good idea," she says. She works at the Trexler Mall, a shopping center just a few blocks from our house. She's the store manager at Fashion Bug. She wants the best for Jay and me, but she knows college tuition will strain our finances.

The high school football coach even calls my mom. Where's Marty? He asks her. Why isn't he at practice? He's throwing away a chance at a college scholarship, a shot at the big leagues, he tells her. "What is bike racing going to do for him," my coach asks. My mom agrees. Her son is shaving his legs, participating in an unfamiliar sport. She's concerned. My dad is, too. Neither of them knows a thing about cycling.

But I remain determined. I'm 16, and I could go to the Olympics one day.

What can my parents do?

From now on, I'm nothing but a bike racer.

3
BORDERLINE OUTLAW

ONE DAY in high school, I'm washing cars at my dad's dealership, earning money for bicycle equipment, when a blue Ford Torino blows into the parking lot and launches off a grassy 3-foot slope separating the dealership from the house next door. The Torino slides to a stop in the neighbor's gravel driveway.

From the plume of white dust the car kicks up, out steps a bike racer with a scraggly handlebar mustache and a shaggy head of red hair. I look at him in awe. *That's Whitehead*. The Outlaw. Whitehead's antics at the Friday night races inspire even reserved fans to hiss and boo. And he loves every minute of it. He flips the bird to the crowd after crossing the finish line. He's been ejected for hocking loogies at hecklers. And the louder the boos, the more Whitehead seems to win.

"What the . . . !" My dad shouts. He charges over to Whitehead. "Pull a stunt like that again, I'll tear you to pieces," my dad yells, waving his giant hands menacingly. I've never met Whitehead before, but I know that when he's in town, stunts like this tend to occur regularly.

Whitehead lives in California and is in T-Town temporarily to race and hang out with his best friend, Gil Hatton. Together they're Butch Cassidy and the Sundance Kid of cycling. They're crazy as hell, but calculated too. They don't win bike races by accident.

Like Gil, Whitehead grew up in SoCal and learned impeccable

track technique from the masters of the sport, including his dad, Pete, who hails from Scotland. Whitehead known the track racing rulebook better than most of the officials. (Gil jokes that most of the rules are in there because of Whitehead.) Whitehead and Gil are also emotional switchblades. You never know when they might pop open.

On the track, they compete by one ethos: win, crash, or DQ. Mess with them in a race and they'll deal with you in the parking lot afterward. "Never wear sandals to a bike race," Whitehead chastises Gil one time. "You always bring sneakers. You never know when we'll need to fight our way out of here." These are the bike racers I aim to emulate.

· · · · · · · · ·

I tag along with Gil, and now I tag along with Whitehead, too. One day, Whitehead and I are out riding in the hills rimming the Lehigh Valley. We're flying down a long, steep descent, when an old Buick pulls out of a trailer park. It cuts us off, nearly hitting Whitehead.

As he frequently does, Whitehead implodes. He knows what an irresponsible driver can do to a cyclist. He used to ride for Heinz on the Panasonic team. He's pushed Mike Walter's wheelchair.

Whitehead rides up alongside the driver's window and starts screaming at him. The smell of cheap whiskey smacks Whitehead in the face. The driver's drunk and belligerent. He tries to shake Whitehead by slamming on the Buick's breaks. The car screeches to a stop, and I clip the rear end flipping over the trunk and skidding across the pavement at nearly 40 miles per hour. Seeing he's really in trouble now, the driver peels out.

Whitehead's infuriated. He wants to strangle the guy. He takes off in pursuit and sees the car pull into a bar just up the road. Inside the bar, Whitehead notices he's outnumbered. Normally, he wouldn't care. But he knows the driver is in the wrong so he picks up the pay phone and calls the cops. When the cop pulls up, he immediately goes over to talk with the driver. The cop ignores Whitehead. Whitehead can tell, the cop is a buddy of the driver.

"This is fucking bullshit," he yells at the cop. "This kid almost got killed, and you're over there talking to the driver like you're best friends."

"Fuck you," Whitehead tells the cop. He doesn't even file a police report.

Back at my house, Whitehead tosses me in the shower. I've suffered road rash before, but nothing like this. The bloody mess stretches from my cheekbone down to my ankle. Chunks of black asphalt sit deep in the wounds.

Whitehead doesn't know what he's going to do about the driver yet, but he knows how to deal with road rash. "You've got to scrub the shit out of it," he tells me. "Here, bite this," he says, sticking a rolled-up hand towel in my mouth. Then he bears into me with a bar of soap, scouring the blacktop out of my skin.

Later, when my dad sees me looking like a bandaged mummy, he flips out. "Who the hell's responsible?" he says. He wants justice. "Don't worry, I'll take care of this," Whitehead tells my dad. He rides by the bar every day for a week. One day he sees the Buick. He goes back to his house and grabs two bottles of Fast Tack, the toxic glue we use to mount our tubular tires to the rims of our bike wheels.

At 10 o'clock in the evening, Whitehead emerges from the bushes beside the bar. He covers the car in glue from the hood to the dent in the trunk where I hit it. He rings the gas tank with the flammable gel. Then he opens a pack of matches, lights a single stick, and flips it onto the car. The vehicle erupts into flames. A few days later we ride by the bar. The car's still there, melted to the ground. Whitehead never gets caught.

Whitehead's the Outlaw. I become a borderline outlaw. He terrorizes T-Town, but he'll whip my ass if I ever get in trouble. He won't let me make the mistakes he made. Whitehead made the '84 Olympic team, but he never won a medal. I'm 16 and I dream of gold.

If I want to succeed, I'll need to learn how to walk the line that
Whitehead steps over

. . . .

I can't wait for the 1988 season to start. If I race well enough, I can go
to the junior world championships in Denmark that summer. I lift
weights religiously, up to five times a week. I'm 17, a junior at Emmaus
High and starting to build adult muscle on my lanky arms and legs. I can
barely walk following the workouts.

I start my season in the early spring at a series of road races in New
York City's Central Park. One of my best friends from the T-Town
development programs, Tim Quigley, lives in New Jersey, not too far
from the city. Tim's an endurance rider not a sprinter, so there's no competitive animosity. Tim's parents, Eileen and Ed, adopt me into their
nuclear family. They fill in when my parents can't get me to an out-of-
town race, which occurs regularly. They make sure my tires are pumped
and my bottles are full before the races.

The Central Park races have no official start time. The whistle
blows when the sun rises. So Tim's parents wake us up at 4 a.m. to get
into the city on time. It's March and still below freezing at daybreak
when we line up. We rub sleep out of our half-open eyes on the start
line. But we never complain—we'll do anything to race our bikes. Tim
frequently wins the competitions, while I mostly suffer.

When summer rolls into T-Town, the track racing starts in earnest.
I race on Tuesday nights in the Pro-Am competitions. Gil and Whitehead sit in the bleachers, drinking beer and cheering me on. "Yeah, get
'em kid!" they shout when I dust the other juniors and lower-category
adult racers. After I take a sprint, I meet them at the rail of the track
and exchange high fives.

Soon I'm dominating the Tuesday night races, and it's obvious I'm
fast enough for the Friday night pro event—but the track officials are

hesitant to let me ride. On Friday nights, Gil and Whitehead will turn from fans of mine into vicious competitors. They just returned from the Japan keirin circuit, where they racked up more than 50 grand apiece in winnings during just a few months. They brought the former keirin world champ, Belgian Michel Vaarten, back with them. Nelson Vails, who won a silver medal in the sprint at the '84 Olympics, is also a regular competitor on Friday nights. But Gil and Whitehead vouch for me. "Let him ride," Gil says. "He's ready." At 17, I'm racing against some of the best sprinters in the world, every week.

Well before I ever got to race on Friday nights, I fell in love with the atmosphere. I used to collect extra cash by doing odd jobs before the races. I hung the flags and helped park cars in the gravel lot. Now I'm part of the action. When the sun sets on Friday nights, the lights flicker on above the track. Thousands of fans, many of them toting six packs of beer, filter into the bleachers and line the wall at the top of the banking.

The racers prepare for the evening's action in an old red barn next to the velodrome. Some of the pro racers get ready by passing around a joint. I walk into the barn and notice a funny smell. Whitehead sees me and grabs me by the collar. "Don't you ever fucking touch this stuff," he says. "If I ever see you smoking this I'll fucking kill you." Walk the line. Do as they say, not as they do. I promise never to touch the stuff, and I never do.

The racing starts, and I do as they say. Gil says go, and I go. In one of the keirin races, Gil yells at me to jump with a lap and a half left. I shoot a hole between a mass of racers with Gil and Whitehead tight on my wheel and hit my max speed on the backstretch. In the final turn Gil blows around my outside with Whitehead in tow. As he passes, Whitehead chops me. He cuts down the banking before clearing my front wheel, knocking me down onto the apron and out of contention for the finish.

"Nice lead out, kid," Gil says after the race. I just got used and abused, but I'm pumped. I'm no longer peering in on the race from the back straight. I'm part of the action.

· · · · · · · · ·

As I get more comfortable racing on Friday nights, I see how the crowd appreciates showmanship, in addition to speed. I learn to ride with panache and to play to the people who buy tickets. From Heinz, the meticulous German and former pro team manager, and his son Mike, I learn to treat my bike racing professionally. I polish my chrome bike parts to a mirrorlike finish and shine my shoes glossy black. I call it the Heinz treatment. "Respect the sport by respecting your equipment," Heinz tells me. "Don't show up looking like a bum," Mike says.

All the top racers have nicknames. Gil's the Bear. Whitehead's the Outlaw. There's the Animal, and Torch, and Art the Dart. The nicknames describe the riders' racing styles. The fans cheer wildly for their favorite racers, and yell even louder for those they love to hate—like the Outlaw. I aim to earn a nickname too. The other racers sometimes refer to me as the Flying Dutchman and the Toast Master, because I so often burn my opponents, but no nickname really sticks.

Then one Tuesday night I'm racing the keirin against a bunch of other juniors and local amateurs. I'm out of position coming into the last lap, so I open up my sprint early. I dodge and weave through racers coming out of the first turn and down the backstretch. Entering the home straight, I kick again and pass three more riders, winning by the width of a tire. "Wow, you sliced through those guys like a blade," says David Mullica, an older racer who's friends with Gil.

Not bad, I think. From now on, I'm known as The Blade.

· · · · · · · · ·

Every Friday night I race against some of the top adult sprinters in the world. Kids my own age don't stand a chance. That summer I win the match sprint at the Pennsylvania state championships, which entitles me to attend the junior worlds team tryouts in Indianapolis. On the somewhat lumpy Indy track, I establish myself as the top junior sprinter in the country and make the junior worlds team.

Just over a year ago I boarded an airplane for the first time in my life. Now I'm jet-setting across the Atlantic to junior worlds in Odense, Denmark. Odense is a 1,000-year-old port town with narrow cobblestone streets and rows upon rows of old brick buildings. The Odense velodrome mimics the T-Town track—an outdoor oval, 333 meters long with a smooth concrete surface and a grassy infield. The breeze off the North Sea brings a fierce chill to the track.

The coach who accompanies us in Odense, Jim Grills, tells me and the rest of the team to focus on gaining experience for the junior world championship in Moscow next year, my last year in the junior ranks. Grills admits the Russian and German juniors dominate track cycling. I shouldn't expect to medal against them. Aim for a top 15 placing, he tells me.

Once the competition starts, I exceed the coach's expectations by simply qualifying for the sprint tournament. (Riders who don't set a fast enough flying-200-meter qualifying time aren't even seeded in matchsprint tournaments.)

But because my time isn't spectacular, I'm placed against the top rider in the first round, an 18-year-old German named Jens Fiedler. I'm overwhelmed. Typically, I'm the aggressor, but at worlds I race timidly. Fiedler rides away from me, and the rest of his opponents. He wins the junior world championship. I finish 17th overall.

· · · · · · · · ·

At the end of the '88 season, the junior national championships return to T-Town. Though I'm the top-ranked junior sprinter in the country, I still haven't won an official national title. I should win easily, but I face plenty of youthful distractions. The local paper touts my exploits at junior worlds. Kids all over town know my name.

When a local cycling magazine profiles me for junior nationals, I tell them my interests outside racing include my car—a Dodge Daytona Turbo—and girls. I regularly draw attention to myself with typical teenage hijinks. "I'm crazier in my car than I am on my bike," I tell the reporter. Girls line up to ride in my Daytona

Gil and I pull up to the track for practice the day before the match-sprint finals, and a cute girl I've been flirting with spots me. She comes running across the gravel parking lot, barefoot, gingerly hopping across the rocks.

"Marty, what're you doing tonight?" she asks.

"Sleeping," Gil says, glaring at me. But I have different plans.

That night Gil leaves his house after dinner. "Where are you going?" his wife asks.

"To make sure that punk kid didn't sneak out," he replies. He drives by my parents' house. My car's not there, so he parks down the street. He watches me pull back in past midnight.

The next day Gil asks me what time I went to bed.

"Early," I tell him.

"Bullshit," he says. I'm busted. Gil lays into me. He won't let me make the mistakes he made. He was a junior world champion, on track to race in the Olympics, and he threw it away. I vow not to let social temptations jeopardize my performance again.

Despite the late nights, I go on to win the 1988 junior national championship for match sprints. I look forward to 1989. I plan on bringing home my own junior world championship medal.

· · · · · · · · ·

On the weekends that I'm not racing, Jay and I stay with my dad, out at his cabin. My dad realizes he nearly lost his two youngest sons when my mom kicked him out. He doesn't booze as much anymore. He makes time for his kids. He wakes us up early and has us do chores around the property. We clear brush and chop wood for the upcoming fall and winter. My dad teaches Jay and me the value of hard work.

When we finally finish the chores, we get to play. We fish for bass and crappie in the lake behind my dad's cabin. Jay and I catch turtles and snakes just for the challenge, then throw them back. My dad tows us up and down the lake behind his rickety motorboat. We tell him to crank up the speed. "Faster, faster," we yell, laughing wildly as we wipe out in a tangle of arms and legs.

Every fall my dad loads us up in his truck. We drive north of the Lehigh Valley, up into the Endless Mountains of Pennsylvania's Bradford County—my family's traditional hunting grounds. The first day of deer season falls on the Monday after Thanksgiving. Rural Pennsylvania schools give kids the day off—because none of them would be in attendance, anyway—but my dad lets Jay and me skip a few extra days of class to try to bag a buck.

For me, life revolves around two seasons: bike racing season and hunting season. While my dad may not offer much support of my early cycling endeavors, he turns me into an adept outdoorsman. I fibbed to get my first hunting license at 11 years old. Our family's hunting lineage spans three generations. We camp out with my dad's brother, Earl, and a crew of friends with whom they've hunted for more than 30 years.

My dad gets up 3 hours before the sun rises over the low-slung mountains and makes a breakfast of eggs and scrapple, a fried Pennsylvania Dutch breakfast side made of pork scraps, cornmeal, and spices. Then we hike into the woods. We head for our ground blinds, made out of loose branches and brush, and sit motionless in the cold morning air. I hold my rifle at the ready, waiting for a buck to enter my range. We wait, and wait, and wait. Patience, my dad says. The buck will come to you. I hear sticks crackle under deer hooves. I see a group of does. I can't wait to fire. Patience, my dad says.

The buck follows them. I count the points on the buck's antlers. *One, two, . . . six, a worthy kill.* I nestle the riflescope up to my eye and cradle the butt firmly above my armpit. One deep breath in. One deep breath out. The crosshairs line up just behind the buck's shoulder blade as it saunters through the trees. I take another breath. The buck stops and swivels its head side to side. It stiffens, sensing danger. I squeeze the trigger. The buck drops to the forest floor.

At night around the campfire, my dad and all the old PA Dutch men slap me on the back. Between their big German hands they pass a bottle of scotch. The flames crackle and hiss as I sit and listen to them talk. Most of what I know about being an outdoorsman—about being a man—I absorb from these woods, sitting around this fire. I learn more on these hunting trips than in any classroom.

. . . .

In the spring of 1989, I'm finishing my senior year of high school. I've grown into my lanky limbs. In the gym, I can squat 400 pounds. At 18, I'm becoming one of the fastest guys on Friday nights, but I still let more experienced riders outmuscle me in the final laps. Because the spectators love the contact, and the racers know how to handle their bikes, the officials let the riders get away with murder on Friday nights. Hooks, shoulders, elbows, and headbutts fly with reckless abandon at the T-Town track.

Gil and Whitehead teach me how to hold my own in the rough-and-tumble rush to the line. We hook and chop one another during road rides, and sometimes get so physical sprinting for town limits signs someone ends up sliding across the pavement. One evening Gil and Whitehead take me out for some keirin practice under the lights at the track. They aim to teach me how to bump and jostle for position in the final lap.

They pin me between them and bounce me back and forth. They're having fun, picking on the junior, just as they do in the races. Then I stick a shoulder under Gil, flipping him up and over his handlebars. He hits the track and a big chunk of flesh comes out of his ass. Okay, Gil and Whitehead say, keirin practice is over.

I can hold my own against grown men, and I'm a man among boys when I race other juniors. On the day of my graduation from Emmaus High, I meet my local rival, J. D. Moffitt, in the finals of the senior state track championships. We'll receive our diplomas in a ceremony at Emmaus High that evening, but first we'll battle on the track.

Both of us qualified for the '89 junior worlds team earlier in the spring, and are slated to race for world championship medals in Moscow a month from now. This race is for local bragging rights—which we take more seriously than any world title.

In the first sprint, I give J. D. a hook in the final turn, just as on Friday nights, and cruise across the line uncontested. The officials relegate me and give J. D. the win. I'm livid. Under the lights on Friday, with the fans watching, the same official would never relegate me, but against another junior, they accuse me of dangerous riding.

I have to win two sprints in a row now. But it shouldn't be a problem. I already beat J. D. in the junior state championship earlier that afternoon. In fact, J. D.'s never beaten me in a match-sprint competition. He's a kilo rider, incredibly fast over three laps, but if I'm anywhere near him when I see the finish line, I win, every time.

We get ready for the second sprint. I see J. D. whisper something to his dad, who's holding him on the start line. The official blows the whistle. J. D.'s dad gives him a huge push. J. D. takes off from the gun. It's a suicide move, but J. D. puts his kilo talent to use. I can't catch him. He beats me for the first time, ever. If I rode J. D. clean the first ride, I would have won without any trouble. I'm a faster sprinter than J. D. I didn't need to hook him. But for some reason, I did. I couldn't control my aggression. That evening I get my diploma, but I still have a lot to learn.

· · · · · · · · ·

The trip to Moscow is a logistical nightmare. We lay over in Helsinki and learn the Feds failed to secure us visas for travel within the Soviet Union. We're delayed an entire day before McDonough convinces the airline to let us on the plane. He tells the flight officials our visas await us in the USSR. After we finally land in Moscow and get visas, we're told the last bus already left for the night. Somehow, someone finds an old rust bucket of a bus for us. We throw our gear inside and head for the Ukraine Sports Complex Hotel.

Rain beats down on the bus as we drive through a dingy industrial landscape. Water splashes up through the wide cracks in the bus floorboards. We finally pull into the worn-down hotel at 3:30 in the morning. The coaches planned on giving us nearly a week to acclimate to the time change and recover from jet lag. Now we need to prepare for competition in just a few days.

The food the race organizers provide us is nearly inedible. At dinner we sit down to bowls of a gelatinous substance filled with fish heads and soup made from animal tongue. We survive almost entirely on food we brought ourselves. I luck out and room with Tim Quigley, whose mom loaded him up on comforting junk food like peanut butter cups, cookies, and sugary instant oatmeal.

Everywhere we go Soviet citizens pester us to trade our American goods. They want blue jeans and Walkmans. They knock on our doors in the morning, before the coaches come to wake us. They're desperate to trade Soviet currency for American dollars.

The low-pressure mentality we took to Denmark last year is gone. The coaches expect us to bring home medals, but more than anyone, we put pressure on ourselves. This is my last chance to compete internationally as a junior—my final shot at scoring a junior worlds medal before moving to the big leagues in the senior ranks.

· · · · · · · · ·

Over the last few months, I've gotten close with of one the girls on the junior worlds team, Christi Fugman. Christi is 16, blond, and cute. She's 5 feet 3 inches and barely 100 pounds. But she's already one of the best bike racers in the country, among both the junior and senior ranks. She lives near T-Town, in Schnecksville, and her dad started her in the Air Products developmental program when she was only 8 years old. (The minimum age to enter the program is 10, so, just as I did to get my hunting license, she fibbed.)

Christi used to consider me a cocky brat and generally ignored me,

but we've become good friends over the last year. Technically, we're dating (whatever that means for high school kids), and she seems to understand me better than most people. I open up and relax around her. The
aggression I feel when I compete melts away. Christi's possibly more
competitive than me. She's tough as nails and has a fierce temper. I don't
mess with my mom when she's pissed. And I don't mess with Christi,
either.

One morning the team heads out for a warm-up spin on the
crummy roads near our hotel. I shout out Christi's name. I need her
attention. I have something really important to tell her, I'm sure. As she
turns her head to look back at me, the road disappears in front of her.

Christi rides off a 2-foot drop where the road inexplicably ends and
crashes. I brace myself for her temper. But she pops up, more embar-
rassed than upset. "I'm okay," she chirps. She's supposed to compete in
the points race that evening, and in the road race a few days later. But
her elbow swells up to the size of a softball. We all know it's broken, but
no one says it out loud.

"I think it's just bruised," Christi says. I feel awful, but Christi lets
me off the hook. She jokingly blames me for breaking her elbow. Amazingly, she still races, though she can barely grip the handlebars. She
finishes mid-pack in the women's road race.

· · · · · · · · ·

I remain focused on the match sprints. I'm setting blazing-fast training
times and anticipate a personal best at the track here in Moscow. The
indoor Krylatskoye Velodrome was built for the 1980 Olympics, which
the United States boycotted. The smooth wood surface is made from
Siberian larch. Its nearly 30-foot-wide banking rises steeply from the
apron like a giant wooden wall, towering above racers riding down in
the sprinter's lane.

Dropping off the top of the banking down to the straightaway during my qualifying ride is like racing down a ramp from atop a three-story building. I nearly spin out of my gear before even hitting the homestretch. Across the finish line, the clock reads 10.5, a personal best and the junior national record at the time. The time holds up for sixth overall and seeds me well in the tournament. Everyone on the team is impressed.

An Italian named Gianluca Capitano wins the qualifier, riding two-tenths of a second faster than me. The Soviet team qualifies their riders second, third, and fourth.

My good form continues into the first round. To narrow the field more quickly, the opening sprint rounds pit three competitors against one another on the track at the same time, instead of just two. The winner moves on to the next round, the losers go to a second-chance bracket, called the repechage. Because of my quick qualifying ride, I face a couple of weaker competitors, one from Poland and another from Italy. Heading into the last lap, I'm out of position, well behind the two riders, and not riding strong tactically. But with my speed I quickly make up ground on them. I sprint across the line in first.

In the second round I run into one of the Soviets and the top-seeded Italian, Capitano. Coming into the final lap I'm in the lead, guarding the front. I refuse to ride tentatively, as in Denmark last year. I race against some of the best in the world every week at T-Town. I'm not afraid of anyone, even the Soviets.

I ride high up on the giant wooden track with the Soviet just above me. If I ride too low, he'll drop off the top of the track with twice my speed and sprint away. But because I'm riding high on the boards, the bottom of the track remains exposed. Capitano charges from behind us, trying to sneak underneath me. I see him coming and fly down the track, bumping him to the apron and stalling his sprint. Whitehead and Gil would be proud. I cross the line first—and am immediately disqualified.

One of the officials is from Italy. He says I rode erratically.

In the repechage, I lose to a Czech rider who goes on to win the silver medal.

. . . .

I'm inconsolable. I worked so hard. I wanted a medal so badly, and it's over, just like that. Tears stream down my face and won't stop. If I'd ridden clean, I could have won. But I didn't control my aggression. I shut myself in my hotel room.

Christi comes to check on me and convinces me I should come down to eat dinner with the team. At the dining table, my eyes are still puffy and red. After dinner, Christi suggests we go for a walk.

She tries to take my mind off the race. Her junior worlds didn't turn out the way she'd planned either. We talk about anything but racing. Around the side of a building we come across a stray German shepherd puppy. We play with the puppy. The pain of my loss eases, I feel better.

. . . .

Back in T-Town that summer, Jim Young, a physical education teacher at the Penn State–Lehigh Valley campus, asks to meet with Tim Quigley and me. Jim's the coach of the university's cycling team, and is garnering accolades from the administration for the national collegiate cycling championships he's winning. Jim knows Tim and I are decent students and, more importantly, some of the best junior racers in the world. He wants us to attend Penn State–Lehigh Valley. We can get a college education and keep racing.

I intend on going to college, but I haven't given it much thought. I'm not certain bike racing is a realistic career track. Tim and I have an outside chance of making the '92 Olympic team, but the games are a full 2 years away. Jim fills out the application forms for us. Sign here, he says. I sign. I'm off to college, to the delight of my parents.

4

BIG BERTHA

AS FALL approaches, I get an unexpected chance at another national title and a potential trip to the senior world championships in Lyon, France. Paul Swift, a 23-year-old sprinter who races in T-Town, needs a tandem partner for nationals. Gil suggests me to Swift as a partner, and Swift agrees. I decide to postpone my first semester of college.

Swift is one of the top sprinters in the country. He's not a natural, but he frequently outduels more talented opponents with tactical guile. I learn from him simply by sitting on the back of the tandem, and pedaling hard.

Both Swift and I bear a grudge against track racing's governing body, USA Cycling—known to most racers as the Feds. The head honchos promised Swift a tandem as a member of Team USA, a trade team composed of the nation's top junior and senior track racers. But the Feds never came through with a tandem for Swift to race, or much other help. The Feds left me completely off Team USA, despite the fact I dominate other juniors nationally. Swift and I aim to prove we deserve better support from USA Cycling at senior nats.

Gil lets us borrow his old Schwinn tandem, a black behemoth that weighs 50 pounds and was built sometime in the late 1950s. Prior to loaning us the tandem, Gil and some friends back in Southern California used it as an around-town cruiser. Swift and I sink $500 into the bike and work side by side getting it back into racing shape.

Once the tandem's up and running, Swift and I take it out to the T-Town track. Something about the bike feels special. It won races before we were born. The heft gives it a solid feeling. We know it won't break down on us, or make it easy for other racers to push us around. We affectionately name it Big Bertha.

· · · · · · · · ·

Tandem racing requires complete cohesion between the two riders. We must perfectly time our movements to keep the bike moving forward quickly, and in a straight line. If we don't jump out of the saddle and sprint in unison, disastrous results will ensue.

I'm taller than Swift—6 feet 2 to his 5 feet 10—and the shorter rider typically sits on the back of the tandem. But because of his racing experience, Swift pilots the bike. He's in charge of steering the tandem and telling me when to jump. As the stoker on the back, I'm the spotter. Like riding in the second seat of a fighter plane, I tell Swift how close our opponents are behind us and on which side they're approaching.

I'm also at the complete mercy of any dangerous maneuver Swift might use to try to win. Swift likes that I'm fearless. I don't freak out; I just hope he doesn't kill us.

At senior nationals in Redmond, Washington, most of the top competitors have trained together religiously. Swift and I only have a couple of hours of practice together before the tournament begins. But what we lack in familiarity, we make up for in speed and tenacity. Swift's a shrewd tactician and a deft bike handler. I boast the limitless energy and ignorance of youth.

At 400 meters in length, the velodrome in Redmond is huge—the size of a running track, but with banked corners. The velodrome's size caters to the big tandem bikes, leaving plenty of space to maneuver. Swift and I will benefit from the long straightaways. We won't need to worry about tactics if we can pedal fast enough.

The tandems go faster than individual bikes, and they can go fast for nearly twice as long. Tandem match sprints take place over 1,500 meters to 2,000 meters, instead of 750 to 1,000 for individual bikes. The sprint on a tandem winds up from as far out as two laps from the finish. Rarely does anyone pass in the final turn.

In the qualifier for the sprint tournament my legs turn like a turbo booster on the back of the bike. I'm eager to erase my disappointing performance at junior worlds in Moscow. Swift points Big Bertha where we need to go. I propel her down the track. We qualify second. Only the defending national champs, Bart Bell and Tom Brinker, beat us.

We dispose of our first two opponents in straight rides and enter the finals against Bell and Brinker. Tandem racing on the velodrome is the cycling version of bumper cars, and Swift prepares for the match by putting on elbow pads and stuffing hip pads into his shorts. He looks like the Michelin Man. I never wear pads. I want the other racers to know I'm not afraid of getting hurt.

In the first ride Bell and Brinker get an early jump on Swift and me. They take off at the start of the first lap and soar out to a demanding gap. The race already seems over as we exit the second turn. But I punish the pedals, and Swift slips Big Bertha into their draft coming into turn three. By the time we exit, he's got the bike even with Bell and Brinker. We cruise ahead as the finish line approaches and win by the width of our front wheel.

On the second ride, Bell and Brinker attempt intimidation. They push us high up the track and try to block us from passing. But we don't wait. We start our sprint with a lap to go and move outside of Bell and Brinker on the back straight. They ride us up the banking of the track. My right arm scrapes the rail at the top of the track and my left shoulder bangs against the opposing stoker.

But Big Bertha holds steady. At 430 pounds of combined weight, Swift, Big Bertha, and I aren't easily pushed around. Bell and Brinker don't realize I thrive on contact. We pound the pedals and exchange elbows. We gain control out of the last turn and fly across the line, battered but not beaten.

I'm only the second US racer to win both junior and senior national championship titles in the same year. (The other racer is Mark Whitehead.) I'm 18 years old and headed to worlds, again.

. . . .

In France, I room with a 20-year-old track racer from Indiana named Erin Hartwell. "Call me Erv," he says shortly after we meet. His nickname dates back to his childhood. Because he was the only white kid playing on an all-black youth basketball team, the other players nicknamed him after Earvin "Magic" Johnson (Erv, for short) to help him fit in.

I quickly learn we've pursued nearly parallel paths in pursuit of Olympic gold. Like me, Erv grew up in a rural, blue-collar community near a velodrome—in his case, the Indianapolis velodrome. He's down-to-earth and hardworking. He sees competitive cycling as a route to a better life.

Even the births of our Olympic aspirations mirror each other. At the age of 7, Erv watched Bruce Jenner win gold in the decathlon. Erv turned away from the television and told his mom, "One day I will be the Olympic champion."

On our bikes, we're both sadists—but in different manners. I enjoy making my opponents suffer during repeated bouts of sprinting. Erv races the kilo. He derives a sick pleasure from self-inflicted agony.

Erv calls the kilo the siren song of sprinting, both beautiful and brutal. He tells me the event's beauty lies in its simplicity: just man and machine clocked over the international standard unit of measurement, 1 kilometer.

The brutality, Erv says, comes from a kilo racer's constant testing of the limits of human physiology. Humans can sustain a sprint, or anaerobic effort, for about 1 minute—or almost exactly how long it takes to race 1 kilometer on a track bike.

During an anaerobic effort, the body produces lactic acid, which the muscles use as fuel in the absence of oxygen. As lactic acid production outpaces the muscles' ability to utilize it, the muscles send a signal to the brain—which the mind interprets as searing pain. Stop. Now. Or you might die, the muscles scream.

Over the course of a kilo race, as lactic acid levels rise and oxygen molecules deplete, the severity of the pain increases. During a kilo effort, a racer feels as if he is receiving a lethal injection of lactic acid.

Erv is built to race the kilo, both physically and mentally. His muscles can quickly absorb and utilize lactic acid better than nearly anyone in the world. He's also adept at ignoring those painful messages his body sends his brain.

Outside of our training sessions, where Erv's deadly serious, he's boisterous—and always up for antics. One of our favorite gags involves prank calling other US riders from the hotel room phone. "Bonjour, monsieur," we say, badly imitating a French journalist. "I would like you to meet in the lobby for interview, and wear your full racing form, s'il vous plaît." Then we race down to the lobby and hide behind a planter. The racer steps off the elevator, fully dressed in spandex with a wide, proud smile across his face, and we laugh hysterically.

Even our differences complement each other. Erv carries himself with an assuredness that others sometimes perceive as arrogance. Confidence is not a facade, he shows me; it comes from thorough preparation. He never lets distractions affect his performance. Control what you can control, Erv tells me.

One day as we're hanging out in the hotel room, Erv and I start talking candidly, and maturely for our young age, about our passion for track racing. "I want to do something positive for the sport after I'm done competing," Erv says.

"Me too," I say.

We decide to chase our Olympic dreams, and then help others achieve their dreams.

· · · · · · · · ·

The velodrome I compete on at the world championships is built on an island park at the center of a little lake in Lyon. The track was constructed nearly 100 years ago and is surrounded by a dense forest filled with mossy vegetation. Its banking and length is similar to the T-Town track's.

Everything about the senior world championships seems inflated, bigger and better than any race I've competed in. The event begins with an opening ceremony and features live TV coverage. The other national teams show off their sparkling new equipment, while I'm given a hand-me-down skinsuit (which I'm asked to return after my race). Even the physical size of the athletes impresses me. I'm clearly a boy among men in comparison to the German and Russian sprinters.

I can't wait to perform on the world's biggest cycling stage, but during the qualifying ride Swift and I lack focus. We slowly circle the top track on the laps preceding our flying-one-lap time trial. I wait for Swift's signal. We ride one lap, then two. We should start sprinting, but we don't. We approach the start–finish line and the officials call us off the track. You're done, they tell us. We miscounted the laps. We rode our qualifier at a warm-up pace.

Because we were riding at the top of track, we didn't even trigger the timing strip laid across the sprinter's lane and clock a qualifying time. The officials could take pity on us and seed us last in the tournament. They could give us a reride. But they don't. They disqualify us. We're sent home from France without even racing.

· · · · · · · · ·

In the spring of 1990, I start college and try to forget about the disastrous worlds trip. I like college, but I don't like college. I major in secondary education and enjoy the business classes I take, but while I should focus on lectures and taking notes, I think only about bike racing. At my current rate of progression, making the '92 Olympic team is a feasible objective. I dream about winning an Olympic gold medal, not economics.

My buddy Tim Quigley moves from New Jersey to Trexlertown so he can attend classes and race at the T-Town velodrome more easily. My mom offers Tim a room at our place. Tim insists on paying $100 in rent. She reluctantly agrees.

As the fall weather turns from balmy to brisk, it gets even harder for Tim and me to concentrate during class. Winter is coming. Soon layers of snow and ice will cover the Lehigh Valley roads. Our opportunities to ride outside are diminishing. Sunlight streams through the classroom window. "This is killing me," I tell Tim. "Let's go ride."

For me, the collegiate races seem like a step backward, too. I'm accustomed to top national and international competition. Instead, I race against a meager group of kids going to class full-time and racing track. Additionally, the coach, Jim Young, sees I'm not buying into his system.

By the end of the semester, I'm yearning to resume racing against the best in the world, and my enthusiasm for school is waning.

· · · · · · · · · ·

In the summer of 1990, I resume tandem racing with Swift. I'm continuously making progress as an individual sprinter. The previous year I placed eighth in the match sprint at senior nationals, and I opened this season's Friday night races at T-Town by winning the keirin final. But racing the tandem allows me to face the top international sprinters, an invaluable experience.

In June, ABC-TV comes to T-Town for an event called the US Olympic Cup. The network is ramping up their coverage in advance of the '92 Olympics and will broadcast the tandem finals live from T-Town on a Sunday afternoon. A host of international stars fly in for the race, including the three-time defending world champions on the tandem, Frenchmen Frédéric Magné and Fabrice Colas. Swift and I want redemption from last year's world championship flop. Now's our chance.

We face Magné and Colas in our first-round match, during the preliminaries on Friday night. Instead of a best-of-three format, the winner of just one match moves to the next round. The French duo leads off the start line. But they don't want the front, and try to force Swift and me into the lead with a track stand. It's a psychological ploy as much as a tactical maneuver. Swift doesn't relent. He halts our tandem beside the French pair.

We sit, motionless, for what seems like minutes. But the experienced French team's bike handling bests ours. We lose our balance and topple over onto the track. Magné and Colas smirk. A few giggles come from the crowd. The reigning US national sprint champion, Ken Carpenter, runs out and helps us back up. He pats my back.

The officials order a reride. I was tense and jittery before the fall. Now I'm pissed. We start the reride. Magné and Colas jump us with one lap to go and open a gap the length of an entire tandem. Swift and I don't give up. We hammer the pedals and gain on them along the back straight. We're even in the final turn, and shoot to the lead with just 50 meters to go. In the photo finish, I'm raising my arms as we cross the line. Magné and Colas come in several bike lengths behind us. We forget about Lyon, France.

Magné and Colas win their way out of the repechage and Sunday, on live broadcast TV, we meet them in the finals. They lead off the line again, and again try to force us to the front with a track stand. This time Swift rides past them and into the lead without stopping. The French shadow us as we creep along the top of the track.

With two laps to go, Magné and Colas drop underneath us and start to wind up their sprint. Swift sticks to their rear wheel. Before the race, Gil told us to go underneath if they leave the door open, and that's exactly what we do. Magné and Colas come out of the turn too high, expecting us to pass on their right. The sprinter's lane opens up. It's like the Red Sea parting in front of Moses. *Holy crap, there's the move.* We dive underneath them. Magné and Colas look at us with exasperation as we pass on their inside. They jump again. But it's too late. They can't catch us. They fade.

I cross the line on the back of the tandem, looking into the stands and soaking in the cheers of the roaring crowd. We just beat the world tandem champions. We wave American flags on our victory laps.

· · · · · · · · ·

Despite the big win with Swift, and my continued progression as an individual sprinter, I feel aimless. To make ends meet, I work part-time at Schuylkill Valley Sporting Goods. In the off-season, Gil gets a job there, too. We sell shoes and stock shelves, but we goof off a lot too. The general manager is a buddy and he takes us back in the warehouse for impromptu football games when business is slow. "Go long," he yells at me, throwing me the ball where Gil can tackle me into a pile of boxes. I like the job, but like college, I don't love it.

As a junior racer things felt so certain. I imagined a path leading directly to Olympic glory. But I witnessed senior worlds. I'm aware of the gap between my current ability and the top individual sprinters in the world. I can see the years of sacrifice closing the gap will require. I'll need focus to achieve my Olympic dream, but most of all I'll need to persevere. No one will hand me a gold medal. I'll have to earn it, no matter how long it takes. Heck, it might even take another decade to win gold, who knows?

· · · · · · · · ·

At the end of the summer in 1990, senior nationals comes to T-Town. Swift and I repeat our victory in the tandem sprint, still aboard Big

Bertha. We're selected for the worlds team, and head to Japan, where we aim to medal.

For the trip to worlds, Swift and I finally get a new tandem, hand-crafted by Koichi Yamaguchi, a master frame builder from Japan, who now lives in Colorado. The bike is a beauty, glossy white with yellow accents. It's constructed with oversized steel tubing developed in partnership with USA Cycling, specifically for track sprinting.

We arrive in Japan, unload our cherished new tandem, and head to the velodrome to practice our sprint. During one effort, we're going all-out coming into the third turn when a tire fails. Miraculously, the tire stays on the rim. We don't crash. But Swift is shaken up. "We could have died," he says, stone-faced. He can't get the incident out of his head.

It's the last time Swift ever puts his full effort into a tandem sprint. In the first round, he rides scared. We lose and fall to the repechage rounds. In the repechage, we lose right away, too, and fall out of the worlds sprint tournament in only two rides.

Something needs to change. I realize that if I'm going to win a medal at worlds on the tandem, Swift won't be the driver. He's technically proficient, but not willing to risk going on his ass. To drive a tandem aggressively, you've got to be damn near crazy. "You need to drive," Gil tells me.

Back in my room, I ask Erv if he's ever wanted to race tandems. He's fearless, like me, plus, his giant anaerobic capacity makes him perfect for the long sprints tandem racing requires. During practice one day at the track in Japan, Erv gets on the back of the bike and I drive. Swift watches us as we test out the new partnership.

Erv and I click on the tandem as well as we do off it. From now on, I'll drive.

5

THE CROWN PRINCE
OF AMERICAN SPRINTING

ERV AND I start the '91 season by beating a pair of world-class Italians in a tandem tournament at T-Town. We make a great team, but it's obvious our respective futures lie in our individual events. I'm winning with regularity on Friday nights at T-Town, and later in the summer of '91, the Feds select me to race in the Pan-Am Games.

I travel to Havana, Cuba, for the Games. The Pan-Ams are akin to the Olympics of the Western Hemisphere. It's my first opportunity to represent my country at a major, multisport competition. I'm given my first glimpse of what it means to be an Olympian. The event is a congregation of some of the best athletes in the world, not just the best cyclists. No one asks me to give my skinsuit back. Instead, I'm loaded up with USA-branded clothing and gear bearing the official Pan-Am logo.

Cuba provides an especially striking introduction to an event of this magnitude. On the evening of my semifinal match in the sprint tournament, the Cuban pursuit team is also scheduled to face off against the Americans for the gold medal. No one in Havana wants to miss the race. A passionate, rowdy Cuban crowd packs the aisles of the national velodrome. Despite sweltering humidity, those who can't get inside the stadium stand 20 deep along the chain-link fence bordering the edge of the track. The musty smell of thousands of sweating bodies fills the air.

I'm warming up for my match when I notice a large military presence in the bleachers. Then, the announcer erupts into a flurry of Spanish over the loudspeaker, enthusiastically shouting, "Fidel Castrooo!" A thickly bearded man wearing a green, flat-topped army cap stands and waves. The crowd erupts in applause. "CUBA, CUBA, CUBA," they chant. The infamous Cuban dictator is watching my race.

I face an Olympian from Argentina named José Lovito in the quarterfinals. I'm accustomed to encountering top international racers at T-Town, but I'm not prepared for the intensity of an event like the Pan-Am Games. Lovito's worked his ass off in anticipation of the Games. I've just shown up. We go toe to toe in three photo-finish sprints. Lovito wins and moves on. It stings. I learn I can compete against the best in the world as an individual racer, but I'll need to work harder to win.

. . . .

After the Pan-Am Games I head to Stuttgart, Germany, for senior worlds. Erv and I aim to win a medal on the tandem. Upon arriving in Germany, we open the door to our hotel room and discover a single king-size bed. Erv and I both stand over 6 feet, and we each weigh more than 200 pounds.

We look at each other. Control what you can control, we think. We build a barrier of pillows down the middle of the bed and go to sleep.

In the tandem sprint tournament we ride well, but not well enough to make the medal round of the tournament. We end up fifth, the highest possible finish outside the medal group. It's my third trip to worlds, and I'm still only 20 years old.

That fall, I decide not to register for classes. I'm emboldened by my Pan-Am performance, even though I was disappointed by the final result. The Olympics are a year away. I want to focus on racing and training, without the stress of midterms and finals.

My parents are pissed. "What will bike racing do for you?" they ask. Cycling isn't a career, they say. I don't argue. I know supporting myself will be a struggle.

I just know I want to win the Olympics one day.

· · · · · · · · ·

In the winter before the '92 season, I tell Christi, "We need to talk." Though we've dated since our senior year of high school, we've always maintained our individual identities. We've never really discussed our future together.

While I've become increasingly committed to cycling over the past year, Christi quit racing after high school. Her decision came as a disappointment to her parents, especially her dad, a cycling nut. Christi's parents stopped supporting her after she stopped bike racing. Now she works 40 hours a week at Prudential Insurance and takes night courses at Cedar Crest College.

As we sit down to talk, Christi braces herself. I rarely approach her so gravely. She's certain we're breaking up. "I want you to know that I love you," I say. "But I really think I could become the best sprinter in the world if I get serious, if I put 100 percent into racing. I want your support, but I also want you to understand, there might be days, weeks when I'm training and traveling and racing, and don't have time for you. I need you to know this is why. I want to be number one."

"Go for it," Christi says. She's seen the top level of the sport, too. She knows the dedication it will take to compete with the best in the world. We're not just a couple of talented kids, having fun and riding our bikes anymore. I'm an adult, trying to make track racing my livelihood. I'm set on achieving my childhood dream.

"I'm here. Don't worry about me. Do what you need to do," Christi tells me.

. . . .

In preparation for the '92 season, I'm in the weight room almost every day, crushing myself. When Erv and I lift together, we end every work-out with a contest we call the backbreaker. We rack 80 percent of our max one-rep lift onto the squat bar and see how many times we can put up the weight before collapsing.

Gil, who's not racing anymore, yells and screams at us as we reach a dozen reps. We strain, wobbly kneed, to put up just one more lift. Then Gil gets in on the backbreaker himself, often showing us up. (Of course, he doesn't do the whole workout before hand.) The backbreaker guaran-tees that we don't cheat ourselves in the weight room. No one will out-work us, Erv and I vow. I leave the gym every day feeling like a piece of scrap iron worked over by an abusive blacksmith.

When USA Cycling snubs me by not selecting me for a national team training camp, I'm only more motivated. The director of the T-Town velodrome, Pat McDonough, one of my coaches as a junior, gets an explanation from the Feds regarding my exclusion from the camp. McDonough says the Feds don't view me as a worthy project. He says the Feds call me an "undesirable."

I pledge to get so fast that the Feds can't refuse me. Then I will set my own terms, hold my own training camps, and invite the riders and coaches I want.

. . . .

I show up to the Olympic Trials in Blaine, Minnesota, in the best shape of my life. My muscles feel twitchy and primed, as if they might pop out of my skin at any moment. Everyone expects me to challenge for the sole Olympic team spot for sprinters, including myself.

Most of the other sprinters focus on just one event. But I'm young, and I have yet to identify my specialty. Gil encourages me to enter a variety of events. I plan on competing in the kilo and match sprints during the Trials, as well as vying for national titles on the tandem and in the keirin throughout the week. But only the kilo and sprints are Olympic events in '92. Win one of them, and I go to Barcelona.

The 2-year-old velodrome in Blaine is a 250-meter wooden track, designed to mimic the Olympic velodrome in Spain. With steep, 43-degree banking and a perfectly smooth surface, it rides lightning fast.

The keirin opens the Trials as an exhibition race for prize money in front of a couple of thousand fans—just as at T-Town. The race also serves as the keirin national championships. Last year, I placed second in the keirin at nationals. This year, I beat Nelson Vails, a silver medalist at the '84 Olympics, and take my first individual national title as a senior. I'm off to a good start.

A few hours later, I line up for the kilo. There's no standard qualifying time required to enter the kilo. Every racer in the country thinks there's a shot at winning the kilo and going to the Olympics. The field of racers fills to 49. I'm one of the early starters.

I tighten my toe straps and rip off four laps around the track as hard as I can. The clock stops at 1:06.69, a track record. Dozens of riders follow me, and none can beat my time. But Erv hasn't ridden yet. He's won the national kilo title 3 years running. Our parallel paths toward the Olympics awkwardly converge. He's my best friend, but I pray that I beat him.

Before Erv lines up to race, the sky turns black and emits a booming clap of thunder. A few sprinkles dot the track surface. Then, the dark clouds open up, and a deluge scatters the crowd. With a handful of riders yet to challenge my kilo time, the officials cancel the race. They'll resume the kilo the following day, we're told.

The track doesn't dry out until the next morning, around when I show up to ride my qualifying ride for the sprint tournament. Everyone at the Trials knows I'm riding well, but they don't realize just how fast I'm going until I nearly beat the reigning king of American sprinting, Ken Carpenter, in the flying-200-meter time trial.

Carpenter is a monster: 6 feet 4 inches and 220 pounds of pure muscle. He's known for his unwavering work ethic and powerful mid-range sprint. He's calm, collected, and relaxed away from his bike, but an absolute terror on the track. He frequently wins races by jumping his opponents as much as 300 meters away from the finish, and holding them off to the line.

Carpenter beats me by just 0.02 seconds in the flying-200-meter time trial. *Hundredths of a second, not tenths!* We essentially ride the same time. In a photo finish, the difference between our front wheels would appear nearly indistinguishable.

I celebrate my second-place seeding in the sprint tournament by clobbering my first- and second-round opponents. Then, I'm told the kilo will start all over. The officials won't count my time against those who didn't get to race. Everyone must compete under the same conditions, the officials contend. If I want to make the Olympic team, I have to race the kilo again.

I need to make a decision. Do I race the kilo and risk tiring myself out for the sprint tournament? Or do I scratch the kilo and focus on making the Olympic team in the match sprint? I ask Gil. "Scratch the kilo," he says. I go all-in for the match-sprint tournament.

The next day I win my quarterfinal race in the match sprints and meet Swift in the semifinal. Swift was seeded fourth in qualifying for the sprint tournament, and if he won his way through the bracket, he'd have faced Carpenter in the quarterfinals, not the finals. So Swift concocted a plan. He intentionally lost and fell to the repechage round. Then he won his way back out, and got me in the semifinals. The winner of our match will race Carpenter in the final.

Swift relies on guile to make up for what he lacks in natural speed. I don't judge him for his racing style. The first wheel across the finish line wins a sprint, not necessarily the fastest rider over the final 200 meters. But I'm unsure what strategy Swift will employ to beat me. He could try anything.

Swift leads the first sprint. After the first of three laps, I come barreling over the top of him, picking up the pace and forcing him to chase me. I want him tired coming into the final 200 meters. Swift catches me shortly after the start of the third lap, and makes a run for my inside coming into the third turn. I move down the banking slightly and we bump shoulders. It's a minor bump, but Swift acts as if I mugged him.

My love tap sends him off the track, past the apron, and onto the infield, where he skids to a stop in front of an official. As I cross the finish line alone, I see Swift gesticulating, waving his hands, and pointing in my direction. He's feigning a foul, like a soccer player who clutches his leg and crumples to the turf but miraculously bounces back up for the penalty kick.

The officials buy his act. I'm disqualified. Swift gets the win. Now I'm pissed and Swift uses my anger to his advantage. I'm faster than Swift, but I'm still young and inexperienced. I can't control my aggression. I win easily, but am relegated, again. Swift makes the finals. My shot at the Olympics is over.

In the gold-medal match Swift and Carpenter tangle on the run to the line on the last of three sprints. Carpenter crashes but is declared the winner when Swift is disqualified. Carpenter makes the Olympic team, but the medal ceremony is delayed. Carpenter is at the hospital getting a 7-inch splinter, a piece of shrapnel from the track's wooden surface, removed from his back. The doctors can only get half the splinter out. Infection will push out the rest, they tell him.

After the Trials, Carpenter asks me to stay in Minnesota and train with him before he leaves for Barcelona. He'll even pay me $500 per week and cover my expenses. I'm honored by Ken's request. Sprinters typically avoid each other. If you want to pummel one another on the track, you don't want to get too close in real life. But Carpenter sees me as the heir to his throne. So far I've proven myself the crown prince of American sprinting. Carpenter will groom me as the next king.

Erv ends up winning the kilo. But my time stands as the fastest of the Trials.

· · · · · · · · · ·

At the Barcelona Olympics, Carpenter places fifth in the match sprint. Erv surprises even himself and wins a bronze medal in the kilo. I stay home and keep training my ass off, while working part-time at the sporting goods store. A month after the Olympics end, Erv and I head to Valencia, Spain, for another shot at the tandem world championships.

The fearlessness Erv and I displayed early in our tandem partnership has faded, and we both know it. We won nationals, again, but witnessed a horrific accident. In the finals of the tandem sprint tournament, Bell and Brinker tried to pass us with only 30 meters to the finish line. Bell steered the tandem to our inside and its front wheel tangled in our rear axle. Their front wheel collapsed, catapulting Bell over the handlebars and into the ground headfirst. He was knocked out, taken to the hospital in an ambulance, and placed in critical condition, remaining unconscious for days before finally recovering. For Erv and I, the accident emphasizes tandem racing's inherent risks. We agree not to make any mistakes at worlds.

Then, during practice one afternoon at the velodrome in Valencia, we're in the middle of a full-throttle 50-plus mile per hour effort when our tandem's rear tire blows out. The track is packed with other riders. I fishtail the tandem up and down the banking, trying to avoid slamming into anyone else, as we struggle to bring the tandem to a stop. The bike handles like a runaway semitrailer on a mountain pass. Finally, after three full laps, we get the bike under control.

Our impetus to race the tandem aggressively is gone. Erv's an Olympic medalist and sees no benefit in risking his life for a less meaningful tandem world title. I'm on the cusp of becoming the nation's top sprinter. I'm certain my own Olympic medal awaits. We've seen first-hand the damage a tandem crash can cause.

So, instead of beating up opponents at worlds, Erv and I wallop each other. We buy a bunch of beach balls and clear the furniture out of our hotel room. We play all-out games of dodgeball, slamming the beach balls off the walls and each other, leaving us exhausted with large welts all over our bodies—but also laughing uncontrollably. It's a hell of a lot more fun than worrying about dying on a tandem.

We repeat our fifth-place performance from the previous year in the tandem sprint tournament, and we're happy to leave Valencia with our skin and skulls intact.

We never race together as a tandem team again.

. . . .

The '92 season ends with one of the world's biggest track races in Paris. The event is called the Open des Nations and takes place over 3 days with nearly a quarter million bucks in prize money up for grabs. I head to Paris as an all-around racer. The Feds figure I can race the kilo or do the flying-lap time trial or help out in the team sprint, a three-person time trial in which the lead rider pulls off after one lap. Carpenter will race the match sprints against some of the world's best, including the reigning Olympic champion, Jens Fiedler.

The Open des Nations takes place at the Palais Omnisports, an incredible structure in central Paris. The stadium's hexagonal shape features sloping walls covered in real grass. It looks like a large upright lawn, a big green pyramid. One of the pursuit riders on the national team challenges the other team members to see how high we can run up the sloping walls. Erv and I charge up the grassy walls outside the stadium, and slide down, getting grass stains on our USA Cycling tracksuits.

On the first evening of racing, Carpenter doesn't seem like himself. His back hurts. He can't sustain his sprint. Before the sprint tournament starts the following evening, he pulls me aside. Carpenter tells me he herniated a disc before the trip to Paris. He can't produce any power.

"I can't do it," Carpenter says. "You have to go."

Fueled by the sudden pressure, I dominate my early-round opponents and make it to the final, where I face Fiedler. The last time we faced each other was at the '88 junior world championships, which he went on to win. Now he's got an Olympic gold medal, and I'm trying to prove I belong among the best.

Carpenter offers me some advice before I head to the start line. He tells me the steep wooden track here will ride differently than the big, shallow concrete track in T-Town. When you transition from the straightaway to the turn on a wooden track, the banking increases dramatically, he says. At low speeds, you're basically riding uphill. Don't get hung up in the corners. Fiedler will attack you, and you won't see him again. Take the front. Pick up your speed entering the turns. Keep Fiedler off balance—speed up, slow down—and most importantly, don't let him pass you.

The race starts. I roll off the start line, out in front of Fiedler. I'm 21 years old, and I'm racing the Olympic champion. I need to keep calm. If I tense up, if I let Fiedler intimidate me, I'll lose. This is the moment I've waited for, my chance to prove I'm number one. I'm determined to seize it.

I crane my neck, keeping an eye on Fiedler behind me. He increases his speed, inching toward my rear wheel. I match his pace so he can't get a running start on me. He keeps coming, faster, faster. He wants to take the front and control the race.

The stadium is packed, but the crowd is quiet, bewildered. Who is this American kid? Fiedler charges my right hip. I heed Carpenter's advice. I won't let him pass. I take a swing at him, throwing him a hook that takes us both up the banking, all the way to the wall at the top of the track. I brush the spokes of Fiedler's front wheel with the back of my bike. The sound echoes through the stadium like a hand sweeping across the cords of a guitar. *Zzzzing.* The crowd lets out a collective gasp. Who the hell is this kid?

Fiedler backs off. We enter the last lap and I keep him high on the track. I won't let him gain momentum for the sprint by dropping off the top of the track. I wind up the sprint and hit my max velocity down the back straight. Fiedler's hung up on my hip as we enter the third turn. He's trying to pass me on the outside, but he doesn't have the speed. I give him a flick. I ensure I keep the lead through the fourth turn, and then, all the way across the finish line.

Yes! I just beat the best sprinter in the world. Everyone is shocked except for me. Fiedler's livid. Who am I to throw him a hook? I'm an upstart, arrogant American kid. He's the Olympic champ. He screams at Carpenter. Carpenter knows Fiedler would've done the same thing if he had the front. But Carpenter also knows Fiedler's the Olympic champ. He suggests I go apologize to Fiedler. I walk over and shake Fiedler's hand. "Sorry," I say, even though both Fiedler and I know I'm not. Then, the officials relegate me. But everyone knows their call is bullshit.

Fiedler garners my apology by virtue of his status as the world's best sprinter. But by not backing down en route to the finish line, I earn Fiedler's respect.

6

ALPINE TRAINING

IN THE WINTER of '93, Gil and I escape the snow and ice and sleet that blanket the Lehigh Valley and travel to San Diego. During the off-season Ken Carpenter had back surgery. Doctors removed part of a disc in his spine. Now, he's getting back into shape, and he asks me to come train with him for a couple of weeks.

Ken treats bike racing as a profession. He goes to bed early and rises before the sun. Every morning, he punches the clock; his satellite offices include the Southern California roads, the weight room where he works out, and the blacktop velodrome in San Diego's Balboa Park where he rides thousands of laps each season.

Ken puts us up in his small, well-kept home. Gil sleeps on the couch. I find a spot on the floor. He turns the lights out at 9 p.m. My tutelage will start first thing the next morning.

It's still dark out when I'm abruptly woken by the sound of coffee beans grinding. I'm 22, and I don't yet understand the drink's magical benefits. The acrid smell nauseates me. Gil gets me out of bed with a kick to the side. "Get up," he says, reminding me I'm still not royalty.

Ken pulls out a giant box of national team cycling clothes from the Barcelona Olympics. He puts on a long-sleeve jersey emblazoned with the Stars and Stripes.

I look at Ken's uniform enviously. Many of the PA Dutch men I hunted with as a kid were veterans of war. Some were even POWs.

72

Around the campfire they told stories about defending our country; they spoke not with bitterness, but with genuine pride. "Listen to and respect these men," my father told me. "Serving your country is a great honor."

I'm no soldier. My country likely won't call upon me to fight in any wars during my lifetime. But when I see Ken, dressed head to toe in the US colors, it reoccurs to me that I can serve and honor my country by representing the United States at the Olympics.

I want to equal, and then surpass, what Ken has achieved. Amazingly, Ken wants to show me how to do just that. He wants me to expand upon what he built. But first I must prove I can do the job required—that I can punch the clock and work from sun up to sun down, every day.

We ride up Highway 101 to Torrey Pines Park, where an abandoned portion of the old Highway 101 gradually winds up a hill overlooking the Pacific Ocean. "Put your bike in its hardest gear," Ken says. I shift into my big chainring, and my smallest cog in the back, a gear ratio typically reserved for steep descents.

We sprint up the gradual hill, again and again. The intense efforts mimic power lifting, but on a bicycle. For up to 3 minutes at a time, I push down on my crankarms with all of my might. I look as if I'm riding in slow motion. I feel every muscle in my legs, ass, and back straining to turn the pedals over, to summit the hill. I gasp for air after each interval.

I've never ridden this hard, this early in the year. For ages, the mentality of many sprinters was to ride around lightly during the off-season, never taxing their legs. They let their big chainrings collect dust during the winter, and subsequently squandered the bulk of fitness they had built during the race season.

Ken doesn't buy into this mentality. "Why would I let myself go from sprinting a 10.5-second flying 200 meters in August to an 11.5 in March?" he asks. Work hard now, Ken says, and race strong all season long.

So we work hard. In addition to the morning rides, we spend hours at the gym every afternoon. Ken is a masochist in the weight room. His daily lifting regimen opens my eyes to the number of plates you can physically stack on a bar before trying to pull it off the ground.

The morning after our Torrey Pines workout (Coffee. Kick. "Get up.") Ken and I ride down to the Fiesta Island training loop. A 4-mile-long, pancake-flat road rings the island, which sits in the middle of San Diego's Mission Bay. Ken describes the morning's workout, a series of 5-minute intervals at 90 percent of our maximum effort. Ramp up the pace until you feel as if you're about to throw up, he says, then hold it.

Ken is smooth and controlled as he flies along the shore of the bay. In comparison, I'm a caricature of pain. By the last minute of each interval, saliva drools from my mouth. Again, Ken says. Then, again.

I'm a mess, but I never falter mentally. I never utter a word of dissent. These workouts got Ken fifth at the Olympics. I want to win the Olympics one day. No one will anoint me the king of sprinting. Ken won't just hand me the crown. I'll have to take it.

The next morning (Coffee. Kick. "Get up.") we go to the track. The velodrome sits within San Diego's 1,200-acre Balboa Park. The park itself is an astonishing place with wide-open spaces, immaculately manicured gardens, and grand museums. But the velodrome, 333 meters long with shallow banking and a number of lumpy cracks, is a dump compared to the silky-smooth surface at T-Town.

Ken tells me the big track is ideal for training, though, especially for building massive top-end power. Its long straightaways allow Ken to turn a bigger gear and reach higher speeds without having to fight the bike through steeply banked turns.

On the Balboa track, my legs acclimate to big gears and high speeds. Ken and I take turns leading each other out for sprints on the long straightaways, one of us ramping up the speed to over 40 miles per hour and the other holding it for as long as he can. Ken developed a reputation for cracking his opponents by outlasting them in drawn-out sprints. I will too.

·········

After my performance at the Open des Nations the previous fall, the Feds declare me their guy for the Atlanta Olympics. They outfit me with top-of-the-line racing bikes and fly me to track events around the world. After the '92 Games, the International Olympic Committee no longer requires racers to maintain their amateur status. I'm free to earn a living from racing my bike. But even for the top bike racers in the US, the term *living* takes on a very literal meaning. My first professional contract, with a team cosponsored by the Philadelphia Flyers, amounts to around $4,000.

It's just enough to pay for the tiny apartment I'm renting from my dad on Trexlertown's sparse main drag, next to our family's Dodge dealership. I put food in my mouth with a stipend from the national team, and one of my biggest motivators, prize winnings. The better I race, the better I eat. The team covers all my cycling-related expenses.

Training, eating, sleeping, and racing are my primary concerns. Results define my success, not salary figures. And as the '93 racing season progresses, my results accumulate.

In March, I compete at the Copa International Championships in Cuba, setting the fastest qualifying time for the flying 200 meters, then going on to win the sprint tournament, as well as the miss-and-out (a mass start race where the last rider across the line each lap is eliminated). I'm named the best overall rider of the event.

In May, I head down to Atlanta for a big-money track race called the First Union Grand Prix. I win and pocket a $1,000 check. Then I'm off to Europe with the national team to race on the prestigious European track circuit.

Over the course a month, I race in Copenhagen, Berlin, and Frankfurt. I'm thrown into sprint tournaments with legendary German sprinters like Michael Hübner and hold my own. At the very first track-racing World Cup, in Copenhagen, I make the sprint finals. I end up with a silver medal after narrowly losing to Italian sprinter Roberto Chiappa.

. . . .

I return home to the Lehigh Valley just in time for the season opener of Friday night racing. Even though I'm the Feds' best-supported sprinter, I must go through the same selection process as everyone else to earn a spot on the worlds team for the keirin.

At the end of July, the Feds hold a keirin tournament in T-Town. The top eight riders in the US will compete in four keirin races, held over 2 days. The two racers with the most points at the end of the tournament will get selected for the keirin at worlds.

In front of my hometown crowd, I win both keirin races on Thursday night, and then secure the first race of the evening on Friday. Heading into the final race of the tournament, I have 12 points and am guaranteed a worlds spot. The four racers behind me, battling for the second selection spot, are all tied with two points each. Among those racers are Swift and Carpenter. Ken never fully recovered from his back injury, and he has struggled in the previous races, but he yearns for a final shot at world championship glory.

I try to repay Carpenter by helping him out in the race. "Stay on my wheel," I tell Carpenter as we start the last selection race. I shoot to the front of the group. But Carpenter lacks the power to stay with me. He gets boxed in and pushed back in the long line of racers. I win my fourth consecutive race. Swift takes second. Carpenter doesn't make the worlds team.

Based on his Olympic performance, Carpenter's an automatic selection for the match sprint at worlds. But he declines the spot. "I have to be honest with myself," he says.

He doesn't race in the United States again. I've earned his crown.

· · · · · · · · ·

We arrive in Norway for worlds. The races take place inside a giant sports arena built in advance of the '94 Winter Olympics in Lillehammer. The velodrome is wooden and 250 meters around. Though the smaller track is not necessarily ideal for big, powerful sprinters like me, the size and surface indicates a trend for international events. I'll need to adapt if I want to remain competitive, long term.

Though it's only August, it's already brisk in Norway. The weather reminds me of fall back home in the Lehigh Valley. I look forward to putting on leg warmers and a jacket for our light training rides through the Norwegian countryside. The cool air invigorates me. I'm confident in the form I displayed all season—undoubtedly the result of hill sprints up Torrey Pines and the vomit-inducing intervals around Fiesta Island.

In the match-sprint tournament, I qualify sixth. I make it through the first two rounds and the quarterfinal relatively unchallenged. In the semifinal match, I meet Hübner, a giant of a man. He's the reigning professional world champion in both the sprints and the keirin.

The winner of our race goes for gold in the finals. In the first sprint, Hübner controls the front and beats me easily. In the second ride, he leads again. I make a run at him through the third and fourth turns, but he's too powerful. I'm close, but he crosses the line half a wheel ahead me.

In the bronze-medal round, I run into another German, Eyk Pokorny. I beat Pokorny in the first ride, but he comes back and wins two straight. He takes the bronze. I finish fourth in the match sprints. Hübner loses to the Australian Gary Neiwand in the gold-medal match.

I finish one step off the podium in my first individual world championships as a senior, and I'm livid with myself. My competitors took advantage of my inexperience and exposed me tactically. I came to Norway hoping for a top-eight finish; now I'm determined to get a medal.

My fourth-place finish doesn't come without reward, though. Fifteen minutes after my bronze-medal race, I'm warming down on the rollers (a stationary trainer preferred by track cyclists) in the national team cabin, when a man in his mid-seventies approaches me. His tells me his name is Jan Derksen, he's Dutch, and he won the sprint world championship in 1946.

Now, he's an agent for the European six-day circuit, a series of track races that take place every winter. The lineage of six-day racing dates back to the origin of the sport of cycling. It's a unique honor to compete in a six-day race, I know. Derksen says the top four sprinters at worlds are offered a spot at the six-days every year. The pay is lucrative, the sprinting mostly for show.

He offers me a contract on the spot. I flip through the document. It's a mixture of languages including Dutch and German, most of which I can't read. But I understand the section that says the contract will pay me $3,000 apiece for three different six-day races in Germany, plus expenses.

I sign the contract.

· · · · · · · · ·

A couple of days later, the keirin tournament starts. In a keirin race, anywhere from five to nine riders race eight laps together around the track. A motorbike leads the group until there are two and a half laps to go. Once the bike pulls off, the racers rush to the finish line.

To ride a keirin is to attempt to control chaos. In a match sprint, I only need to worry about my opponent and myself. But in the keirin, five other racers want me to lose. I've gone from first to fifth in a matter of meters during keirin races. Ride high in the final turn to block someone from passing, and three riders will drop underneath you. In the keirin, a little luck goes a long way.

I plan on avoiding the inherently dangerous fight for position, and continuing to use my dominating long sprint to win races. In the first round, I go to the front as soon as the pace bike pulls off the track with 600 meters to go. I slowly raise the speed, fast enough so that no one is tempted to jump past me, but not so fast that I fizzle out before the final 50 meters. Race after race, no other rider can come around me. I win my way into the keirin finals determined to rectify my mistakes in the match sprint. I eye my competition. Hübner fell in the semifinal and broke his collarbone. He's out. But Neiwand's in the race. He's the uncontested favorite. Two crafty Japanese riders toe the line. They'll try to work together. The Frenchman Magné is a wild card and someone to watch for on the last lap.

Gil isn't in Norway, but I can hear him in my head as I line up. *Battle for the front from the start. Get behind the pace bike. Stay out of the rough surf, the turbulence.* "Rough surf" and "turbulence" are the terms Gil and I use to refer to the scrum of racers battling for position behind the leader, where it's like riding in the choppy white water of a crashing wave, or the disturbed air on the trailing edge of an airplane wing.

The race starts, and I surge off the line, beating every other rider to the front and taking first wheel behind the pace bike. The other riders try to push me out of position, but I fight them off. Just before the pace bike pulls off, a Japanese rider, Toshimasa Yoshioka, rides up beside me with his teammate in tow. I let Yoshioka in front of me and bump my way back onto his wheel, forcing his teammate out of position.

The pace bike pulls off, and I'm second wheel. Perfect. Two laps to go. Yoshioka winds up his sprint. He gets low on his bike, maximizing his aerodynamic profile, hoping he can get going so fast that no one will come around him. The air buffets off my large frame behind the Japanese rider. I'm perfectly positioned to lead with a lap to go.

The bell signaling the last lap rings as we cross the start–finish line. I sense the riders behind me jostling for position, preparing to pounce. We round the second turn, into the back straight. I jump beside Yoshioka.

We're nose to nose as we enter the third turn. Neiwand swings to my right, high up on the banking. He's flying, but he's also taking the longest route to the finish.

We fling ourselves out of the final turn. Less than 75 meters to the line. Yoshioka leads, barely. Magné finds a hole along the inside. Neiwand surges. We're four riders wide across the track as the line approaches. 30 meters . . . 15 . . . 10. I pass Yoshioka. Neiwand nips me. Magné throws his hand in the air, unconvincingly.

The replay confirms Magné passed Yoshioka on the blue apron, the equivalent of running out of bounds en route to a touchdown. The officials disqualify him. We're still spinning around the track, cooling off from the dramatic finale, when Neiwand is announced as the winner. I move up to second. I'm a silver medalist at the world championships. A step away from number one.

· · · · · · · · ·

I break through at the world championships, but Erv regresses. After winning a bronze medal at the Barcelona Olympics, he finishes sixth in Norway. He's disappointed in his performance and determined to regain his prominence among the top kilo riders in the world. He convinces the Feds to send him to Australia for the winter. There, he trains under the national team director Charlie Walsh, whose drill sergeant–style coaching put Australian cycling atop the world rankings.

After his 3-month stint in the Southern Hemisphere, I reconnect with Erv at a US national team training camp in Alpine, California. We're the only sprinters at the camp, which is primarily for road racers and endurance track riders. We choose to ride in the mountains while the other sprinters on the national team stay at an oceanfront rental house in Huntington Beach.

It's only January and Erv is already riding stronger than anytime in his life. He tells me about excruciating days on the bike in Australia, under Walsh's coaching. The atmosphere was akin to a cycling boot camp, Erv says. The Australians put in 600 miles a week, doing 180-mile road rides. Their uphill, big-gear intervals weren't just a few minutes long, but a full 6 miles. They did weight work and super high–intensity sprints on indoor trainers that measured their power output. And since it was summer in Australia, they regularly competed in track races on the weekends as well.

The workload took Erv to the brink and then well beyond what he thought he could endure. He says it's no secret why nearly all of the Australian cyclists he trained with were world champions: hard work and tons of it. We thought we worked just as hard as everyone else in the world. We were wrong.

If we want to beat the Australians and the Germans and the French, we need to work harder. Miles, we need miles. Fitness is like a pyramid with aerobic endurance at the base, Erv explains. The bigger the base, the higher the peak. To sprint faster as the season progresses, we need volume now.

With that mentality, we go full-throttle at the Alpine training camp. The endurance riders are the Indy cars of the bike racing world, made to go 500 miles at a time. We're the dragsters, built for a quarter mile, blazing fast. Everyone expects us to roll over at the feet of the endurance riders, who possess double our aerobic ability. But instead, we terrorize them.

We wake up every morning well before the sun crests the densely forested mountains surrounding Alpine, a little town just east of San Diego. It's the height of the WWF craze and we get a kick out of imitating the wrestler Rick Flair's trademark, "Woo!" Erv and I walk down the hall, knocking open the doors of the other riders and sticking our heads inside the dark rooms. "Woo!" we shout, rousing them from bed. We bang open door after door, shouting all the way down the hall, "Woo! Woo! Woo!" It's a fine, positive start to the day.

When we roll out with the endurance team for rides, Erv and I start in an all-out sprint, right from the parking lot, even though our legs ache from the previous day's workouts. The groggy endurance riders scramble to catch up with us. When they do, they look at us with sneers, annoyed we made them suffer so early in the ride. But we're determined to get in our licks while we can. We sprint away from them at stop lights, too, trying to make the skinny endurance riders suffer before the road points upward, and we start to fall to the back of the group.

On the climbs, we heave as the endurance team chats casually. Erv and I just aren't designed to go uphill. Not only are we carrying 50-plus more pounds than the scrawny pursuiters and roadies, but our fast-twitch muscles crave short, rapid-fire bursts, not the slow burn that the prolonged mountain roads surrounding Alpine dish up. But we never give up on a climb. To stay with the group we claw and scrape and suffer until our eyes start to roll back in our heads.

Other US sprinters think we're nuts for riding this much, this hard. But road rides aren't all we do. In the afternoons we regularly hit the weight room, lifting until we feel queasy with exhaustion.

Each day, when we get back from the 100-plus-mile rides, the terrorization continues. We strip off our cycling clothes and launch into the hotel Jacuzzi buck naked. We organize impromptu games of tackle football and pull all sorts of hijinks.

"Stop talking about bikes," Erv says one day to a rider who's fretting about the next day's 7-hour ride. "You're stressing me out. It's going to be 7 hours tomorrow, and the day after that, and the day after that. Accept it and move on." Control what you can control, Erv says.

No one works harder than Erv on the bike or in the gym. But when he's not training, Erv makes a point of enjoying himself. We're each given a reasonable stipend during the camp, and Erv blows through his money in just a few days, spending it on gourmet meals, expensive drinks, and an array of newspapers. I'm more fiscally prudent than Erv, but I share his mentality. Training is deadly serious. Everything else should be fun. Let's laugh. We're still kids.

On one of the final days of the camp, we roll out into drizzling rain and 50°F temps. We ride and ride and ride. The road snakes up through a mountain valley and over a giant pass between two snow-capped mountain peaks. Eventually I tail off the back of the group. The other riders prance up the mountain in front of me as I struggle to keep them in sight. The US national team coach, Danny Van Haute, pulls his follow car beside me.

"How much longer to the top?" I ask.

"An hour," he says.

I dig in. As the summit nears, I start to pass some of the roadies who cracked and gave up. I crawl over the crest of the mountaintop and reintegrate with the group on the descent. *Always sprint through the line,* I think.

The final climb of the day comes in the last few miles, winding up a hill to our hotel in Alpine. I ride next to Erv as we lug our way up the last long climb. We're cold and exhausted. Our sopping wet clothes hang from our limbs.

We take pride in the way we suffered, in how we're suffering right now. The tenacity we put into every bike ride. Every pedal stroke, we turned with purpose. I look over at Erv. Water streams off the tip of his nose. His eyelids appear blue. He looks back at me. We grin at each other. Shit, '94 is going to be a good year.

· · · · · · · · ·

During the camp in Alpine, the Feds hire a new national team coach for the sprint program. When the Feds had asked me earlier who I wanted as my coach, I had suggested Andrzej Bek, who came highly recommended by Ken Carpenter. Bek is also a friend of Eddie Borysewicz (Eddie B, for the tongue-tied), a fellow Polish immigrant who transformed the US cycling team into a dominant world power during the '80s. Andrzej's Eastern European mentality doesn't tolerate weakness.

He only comprehends hard work and results. He commands respect and reciprocates it to those who are deserving.

Under Andrzej, the team's workload doubles. He combines a huge volume of time on our road bikes with brutally intense workouts on the track. Many of the national team riders fall by the wayside. Some can't mentally handle the training and quit. Others simply break down physically, succumbing to fatigue or suffering debilitating overuse injuries. But Andrzej doesn't flinch.

The training is necessary to create a team of Olympic-caliber athletes. But it's also his way of cleaning house, weeding out the weak, and leaving him with a group blessed with both the mental will and athletic potential to succeed. I never flinch or waver. I gobble up the training Andrzej dishes out, and remain hungry for more.

Andrzej recognizes this, and we develop a deep bond based on mutual respect. This is the man who will take me to the Olympics. I am the athlete who will validate his career as a coach. He tells me I can win the Olympics, but I will have to work harder than anyone in the world.

· · · · · · · · ·

In the spring of '94, I return to T-Town and continue training under Andrzej's direction. Everything is going according to plan. I'm faster and more focused than anytime in my life. Then, one day, Christi calls me. "We need to talk," she says. It's unlike her to be so serious. I'm concerned.

We sit down, face to face. She gulps. Her eyes are glossed with tears.

"Guess what?" she says with a somewhat forced chirpiness. "I'm pregnant!"

She's 21. I'm 23. We've mentioned marriage offhand. Kids? Never.

She's scared—more scared than at any time in her life. She took the pregnancy test four times. *It's wrong, it's wrong, it's wrong, it's definitely wrong*, she thought. But each time the test came back positive. Then she went to the doctor for a blood test. The test is right, the doctor says. This can't be happening.

But Christi's happy, too—happier than she could ever imagine. She loves me. She wants this child. She wants a child with me.

"What do you think?" Christi asks me, biting her lip.

"Okay . . . okay," I say. *Okay, I can do this*, I think. "Okay, we can do this," I say.

Despite the pregnancy, we decide to stick to our plan. The goal is the Atlanta Olympics. We decide to postpone getting married until after the Games—until I accomplish the goal. Christi knows how she feels. She wants to be with me. I love her. I want to be with her. We don't need a ceremony to prove that.

But we do need money. My priorities remain training, eating, sleeping, and racing—but now, supporting a family as well. My current salary won't cover diapers and formula. To keep my Olympic dream alive, I need to win.

· · · · · · · · ·

At a Friday night race in June, T-Town hosts the International Madison. The Madison is one of track racing's oldest endurance events. The name comes from the race's best-known venue, Madison Square Garden in New York City. Europeans simply call the race, the American.

In a Madison race, teams consist of two racers who take turns competing. While one racer competes, the teammate recovers by circling the top of the track. The teammates switch off every lap or two. The one who's racing will grab the other's hand and then sling the teammate up to speed, into the action of the race.

The Madison is an exciting but sometimes dangerous event. Teams win by accruing points at the finish of designated laps. The point system makes for constant action within the race, with riders jockeying for each upcoming sprint, or trying to break away from the pack and lap the field. And because the relief system lets the racers rest between their sprint efforts, the speeds stay consistently high throughout the race.

But the regular and unscripted exchanges between teammates make for a chaotic pack of riders. Throughout the event, racers must navigate a minefield of relief riders traveling a fraction of the pack's speed. Additionally, muffed hand slings between teammates often end with both racers sprawled out across the track, along with anyone unlucky enough to come up behind them.

Even though I'm considered a sprinter, and technically not suited for the 80-lap Madison races, the high speeds and handling skills required in the event make it my type of race.

But Gil disapproves of me racing any events other than the match sprints and keirin.

"Why risk it?" Gil says of the oft-sketchy Madison races.

"Because I'm going to win, and I need the prize money," I respond.

Thanks to the hard work I put in over the winter and spring, I'm experiencing my best season yet. I've backed up my breakout keirin medal at the '93 worlds with impressive performances on the World Cup circuit, and I'm currently the third-ranked track sprinter internationally. In the US, I've regularly been competing in, and winning, a variety of endurance races on the track.

For T-Town's International Madison, featuring teams from around the world, I partner with a rider a couple of years younger than me, Ryan Oelkers. Ryan is the nephew of T-Town's first director, Jack Simes. He comes from a lineage of top professional bike racers on his uncle's side. In fact, Ryan's grandfather, Jack's dad, actually competed at Madison Square Garden during the golden era of track racing in the 1920s and '30s.

Though he's small, red-headed, and freckly, Ryan's New Jersey upbringing gave him a quick tongue and instilled in him a take-no-shit attitude. I like his toughness. Though he wasn't officially invited to the Alpine training camp, Ryan showed up anyway and slept on the floor in a hotel room the national team used for equipment storage. He's one of my best training partners, always game for a long winter ride in subfreezing temperatures. And while he might not possess world class talent, Ryan's a tenacious competitor, willing to dig deeper and suffer more than most racers. We're great friends.

Ryan and I warm up for the Madison by practicing a few hand slings on the track. I fly up on Ryan's inside and reach for his outstretched left hand. His fingers are turned toward me, ready to clasp my own. I grab Ryan's hand and hold on tight as I continue forward, sailing in front of him. My momentum slows as he builds up speed. I fling my right arm forward, shooting Ryan in front of me.

But as Ryan comes past me, the curve of his handlebars tangles with mine. We're grasping our bikes with just one hand each and can't keep them stable. Ryan's front wheel veers in front of my bike. He slams into the track surface and I'm thrown into the air, performing an uncontrolled front flip up and over him.

My lower back hits first as I come crashing to the ground, followed by my ass, and then my legs. The momentum of my fall causes my left heel to whiplash into the track, hitting the concrete with an audible smack. Pain shoots through my heel and radiates up my Achilles. It feels as if someone drove an ice pick through the sole of my shoe. Instantly, I know something's broken.

I try to stand up, but I can't put any weight on my left foot. I'm carried to the medical tent, where the T-Town EMTs put ice packs on my heel and tell me it's just bruised. No, it's broken, I tell them. I broke my heel. That's impossible, they reply. Construction workers who fall off 50-foot buildings and Indy car drivers who slam into the wall at 200 miles per hour break their heels, but not cyclists.

My old friend, Tim Quigley, who's now an intern at the T-Town velodrome, appears at my side. Tim and his brother carry me to Tim's car and take me to the hospital. An x-ray reveals I split my calcaneus, the squash-shaped bone that composes the heel. The bone is the support structure of my entire foot and lower leg. The break looks as if someone took an ax to the fat end of the squash, nearly shearing it in half.

A local orthopedist who was the US national team physician at the '84 Olympics, Dr. Tom Dickson, is on call at the ER and treats me. Dr. Dickson says orthopedists refer to such injuries as an aviator's fracture. The term comes from the 20th century, when crash landings could crack a pilot's heels as the heels were driven into the airplane rudder. That's the type of force it typically takes to cause this kind of injury, Dr. Dickson says.

Doctors frequently refer to a calcaneus fracture as one of the most painful breaks a human can suffer. Any impact hard enough to break the bone must first get through an inch-thick layer of soft tissue that encapsulates and protects the heel. The traumatic hemorrhaging of this tissue causes the majority of the pain.

Before placing me in a cast, Dr. Dickson packs chewing tobacco against my skin. He tells me it will draw out the blood and alleviate bruising and swelling in my heel. Then he wraps plaster around my foot and lower leg. The cast rises from my foot to just below my knee. The tobacco stings where it presses against the fresh road rash on my leg, and a smelly fluid oozes out from the cast.

I'm told that when my cast comes off in 4 weeks, my heel will still hurt. But as long as I can endure the pain, I can ride. I'm not so sure, though. My heel is swollen up like softball. I can't walk. How will I even fit it into a cycling shoe? How will I sprint?

Later, I air my frustrations to Tim. Worlds is just 6 weeks away. I was flying, in the best form of my life, and now I'm done. I'll never recover in time to compete, to prove I'm number one. But Tim won't hear it.

He dreamed of riding in the Olympics one day, of winning a world championship. But no matter how hard he worked, and he worked harder than any of us kids, he just wasn't good enough. Tim didn't achieve his dream, but he won't let me lose sight of mine.

"If it's a matter of enduring pain, if anyone can endure it, you will," Tim says.

7

THE FASTEST CYCLIST
IN THE WORLD

FOR TWO WEEKS after the crash, all I can do is upper-body work in the gym and aerobic exercise on a handcycle. I try to maintain my strength, but I can feel the fitness draining out of my body. My left leg starts to atrophy. My muscles wither away before my eyes. I worry that all of the fitness I worked so hard to build up over the winter and spring will disappear.

When the cast finally comes off, I start rehab. My physical therapist, Randy Neri, makes me climb into an arctic-cold ice tub up to my chest. He uses ultrasound to stimulate the bone and tissue and speed up the healing process. Then he has me flex my foot in a series of exercises aimed at increasing my range of motion. I grimace. It kills me. But Neri assures me that the painful therapy will get me back on my bike quicker.

After less than a week of therapy, I start riding again, even though I'm never officially given the go-ahead by my doctor. Through trial and error, we develop a system of taping my foot that causes the least amount of pain when I sprint. The athletic tape completely immobilizes my ankle. I wear a shoe one size larger to accommodate the wrapped ankle, and a horseshoe-shaped pad in the sole that alleviates the pressure on my broken heel.

After a few days, I try an all-out flying 200-meter sprint to test myself. I finish the effort in 10.8 seconds, 0.2 seconds off the time I set before the injury. A significant drop in performance. It's evident that I need more time to recover. An x-ray still shows a large split in my heel, and I can't put any weight on my left foot. Neri has me perform an iso-kinetic strength test, which reveals my left leg is operating with 30 percent less power than my right.

But if I want to go to the Atlanta Olympics, I don't have a choice. I have to race injured. The national championships, just a week away, will serve as the qualifying race for the '95 Pan-Am Games. And the Pan-Am Games are a qualifying race for the '96 Olympics. Only the top two riders from nationals will go to the Pan-Am Games. The current rules don't allow for a selection at the coaches' discretion.

I petition USA Cycling to change their selection process. The Pan-Am Games are 8 months after nationals. It doesn't make any sense to select riders so far out. But the Feds tell me my request is blocked by the objections of one competitor, Paul Swift. Swift knows if I can't race nationals, he has a better shot at making the Olympics. To appeal Swift's objection, the Feds tell me I must go through the elected rider representative to USA Cycling. And oh, by the way, the current rider representative is Paul Swift.

With changing the Pan-Am selection rules no longer a possibility, I must decide between two career-threatening options. The straightest path to the Atlanta Olympics is through nationals and the Pan-Am Games. If I don't race nationals, I narrow my options for getting to Atlanta. But Dr. Dickson warns that my immobilized ankle puts immense strain on my Achilles tendon. If I race, it could completely rip away from the bone during a sprint. I'd never be the same athlete again.

I ask Gil what he thinks. "Let's go kick Swift's ass with one leg," he says. I head to nationals.

· · · · · · · · · ·

I show up in Indianapolis on crutches, and I'm still receiving therapeutic treatments from Neri as often as three times a day. The other racers think I'm faking the injury. You can't even walk, no way you can sprint, they tell me. But before each race, Neri tapes my ankle, immobilizing it. Then I hobble up to the start line, hand Gil my crutches, and climb onto my bike.

By now, I'm accustomed to the pain in my heel. It's as if the pain is a part of me—indistinguishable from the anaerobic suffering I endure in a race. But because rocking back and forth on my injured left foot hurts too much, I can't play tactical games in the match sprints. I lead out every sprint, using my long-range power to beat opponents. The tactic works through the early rounds.

I advance to the semifinal round, where I meet Paul Swift. The winner makes the gold-medal match and earns a spot on the Pan-Am Games team. Swift wins the first sprint. I take the second. Then, as we prepare for the match that will decide our fate, a clap of thunder sounds in the distance. Lightning flashes. Rain pours down onto the track. The officials delay our race.

The longer we wait, the more mad and determined I get. I'm going to throttle Swift. I only came to Indianapolis because of him, and now I can knock him off the Pan-Am team while securing my own spot. I'll win this race even if my Achilles ruptures in two. At midnight, we're finally cleared to line up for the final match.

It's mid-July in the Midwest. The recent rain makes the air inside the velodrome thick and muggy. Moths flutter around the floodlights towering over the track. Swift relies on tactics and guile to win sprints. I rely on the massive base I built during the winter in Alpine and my intense training under Andrzej in the spring. Instead of fading over the course of the sprint tournament, I'm getting stronger. I've regained my form. On the last lap, I take off, leaving Swift in my wake.

I ultimately lose in the finals, but I consider my race against Swift my championship. When the local paper asks me if Swift and I exchanged words, I say, "I told him things come back to haunt you. He left the track crying. I left laughing."

I make the Pan-Am Games team. My path to Atlanta is cleared.

· · · · · · · · ·

I return to T-Town as a swampy heat wave hits the Lehigh Valley. Temperatures soar over 100°F inside the breezeless velodrome, and Andrzej schedules my hardest workouts for the middle of the afternoon, during the hottest part of the day.

His plan is to prepare me for the sweltering heat I'll encounter at worlds in sunbaked Palermo, Sicily. Palermo is one of Europe's hottest cities. In August, the town turns into a veritable furnace.

Riding hard in the heat now will harden me for worlds, Andrzej assures me. But many of the world-class racers based in T-Town think Andrzej's trying to kill me. They won't come train with me, calling the workouts a "death match." So I train alone, my gaze set firmly on Palermo.

Most top-level athletes will rarely acknowledge they ever need a break, but I admit my broken heel forced me to rest and helped me recover from a demanding early season. With my large aerobic base, I bounce right back. I'm in the shape I was before my crash, ready to prove I'm number one.

I show up in Italy still hobbling on my cracked heel. My Achilles aches as well. As Dr. Dickson predicted, the tendon is overcompensating for my continually taped ankle. But despite the constant concern of my injury, I'm inspired by Palermo.

It's an incredible city nestled on the coast and surrounded by mountains. The narrow streets are packed with little Fiats and Vespas. Greasy Italian gangsters with chest hair and big gold chains are everywhere. The Feds caution us to behave respectfully. More bluntly, they say don't do anything stupid. As if we needed any more of a reminder, the velodrome in Palermo is named after a local judge who prosecuted the Cosa Nostra (the Sicilian mafia) and ended up the victim of a car bomb.

I relish the air of danger. Palermo's gangster reputation heightens my senses. I'm on edge, ready to fight. I also like the city's dingy feel. I come back from road rides with a thin layer of dirt caked on my lower legs. It seems like a place where only the hard survive. I truly feel like my life is on the line in Sicily.

The velodrome in Palermo is huge. It doubles as an outdoor sports complex with a full-size soccer field in the center and expansive bleachers that seat up to 15,000 people. The track is 400 meters around. It perfectly suits the drawn-out sprinting style I've developed. As Andrzej anticipated, the temperature inside the stadium is blistering.

The Feds give me a new uniform to wear during my qualifying time trial for the match-sprint tournament. It's the latest in aerodynamic technology, a long-sleeved skinsuit coated in rubber. The material may slice through the air, but as I struggle to stretch the suit over my clammy skin, I realize it doesn't breathe.

The sun bakes the track as I ride my flying 200 meters. I finish my time trial in 10.47 seconds, a personal best for qualifying, then I ride straight to the infield. I'm burning up inside the rubber suit. "Get this thing off me!" I yell as the USA Cycling staff struggles to strip the sticky rubber sleeves off my arms. The suit proves more detrimental than useful. I rode faster flying 200s during practice.

I end up seeded seventh entering the sprint tournament. That means I'll face tougher opponents in the early rounds. I beat an Italian favorite, Federico Paris, then meet another Italian, Roberto Chiappa, in the quarterfinals. Chiappa is a former junior world champion and was fourth at the '92 Olympics. The Italian fans, known as the *tifosi*, go crazy for Chiappa. They chant and bang drums as we line up for our first ride.

"RO-BERT-O, CHI-APPA!" *Boom, boom, . . . boom, boom, boom!*

"RO-BERT-O, CHI-APPA!" *Boom, boom, . . . boom, boom, boom!*

Chant, yes, chant, I think. *I'm about to shut you up.*

The race starts. Chiappa and I swoop up and down the banking, jockeying for position before the bell lap. He leads as we cross the finish line with one lap to go. I push Chiappa from behind, ramping up my speed, and forcing him to increase his own pace to protect the front. The faster Chiappa goes, the louder the crowd roars. Fifteen thousand fans scream as we round the backstretch. I stalk Chiappa as if I'm hunting in the woods. He's in my crosshairs. I wait for the right moment to strike.

We roll toward the third turn on the wide-open back straight. I stand and make a run at Chiappa's rear wheel. Two hundred meters to go. I'm at full steam. Chiappa kicks. The Italian fans yell, straining their lungs. But it's futile. I pull the trigger. Chiappa is dead. I blow by him as we exit turn four. A hush sweeps over the stadium. It's as if someone pulled the plug on a stereo. I cross the finish line alone, in silence. Only the call of the Italian announcer, pronouncing me the winner, fills the void.

Next.

In the semifinals, I meet Hübner. He knocked me out of the match sprint a year before. He wins the first ride. On the second ride, I dive underneath Hübner just after the start of the bell lap. Three hundred meters remain between the finish line and my front wheel. I don't care. I start sprinting, daring Hübner to come around me.

I lean out of the saddle and wind up my sprint. My legs fire up and down like a pair of jackhammers. Hübner waits. He thinks I'm sprinting too early. But by the time he makes a run at me, it's too late. I beat him by a wheel at the line.

"*Uno a uno!*" the Italian announcer shouts over the stadium's sound system. We line up for the tiebreaker. The winner goes to the gold-medal round. I'm emboldened by my long sprint, a product of my superior fitness. In the third ride I employ an identical tactic. I cut underneath Hübner with one to go. I wind up my sprint 300 meters out. Again, I hold him off by half a wheel at the line.

As we cool down, Hübner extends his arm and congratulates me. "Great ride," he says in a strong German accent. "Good luck in the finals." But moments later, I look up at the stadium's scoreboard in disbelief. I'm relegated. Andrzej asks the officials to review the tape. Eight officials watched the race. Just one accused me of erratic sprinting. If they look at the replay and determine I rode clean, I'll race for a gold medal at worlds. If they agree with the sole, objecting official, I lose.

The replay shows I hooked Hübner and flirted with the line demarcating the sprinter's lane as he attempted to pass in the third turn. But the officials rule my aggression doesn't warrant disqualification. I move on to the gold-medal round.

· · · · · · · · ·

In the finals, I face Darryn Hill for the first time in my young career. Hill is an Aussie sprinter who beat Jens Fiedler in the semifinal round. He has an angular face and a mop of frosted blond hair. He's cocky and brash, a lot like me, and when he straps on his helmet, he's known to turn into a total prick. I can't wait to race him.

But I'm also anxious. I've never succumbed to nerves before a race. I've never let a negative thought get to me or doubted that I would win. When I line up, I shut out everything but me and the track and my opponent. I feel as if I'm incapable of losing. And most of the time, I am.

This race is different, though. I've trained for this race my entire life. This is my opportunity to prove I'm number one. I told Christi I was going to be the best in the world, and she believed me. "I'll be here," she said. And she has been.

Now, she's pregnant.

Win this race, and I secure our future. The sponsors and the salary I need to support a family racing my bike will come through. Lose, and I may not even garner a headline in the Lehigh Valley newspaper. For the first time, ever, I feel pressure. And I like it. I want to be the guy holding the ball in the final seconds of the game. I like knowing that people are counting on me.

Andrzej holds me at the start line, next to Hill. I sit upright on my saddle, taking measured breaths, each one a little deeper than the next. With each breath I suck up the butterflies in my stomach, and blow them out into the warm night air. I close my eyes. I see Christi. I see my mom and I see my dad. I see Gil. I see Heinz and Mike. I see everyone who's contributed to my success. *These people are my team*, I think. *They've made sacrifices to help me become number one. Don't let them down.*

I take one big, final breath. I hold the air inside. I puff out my cheeks and exhale with all my might. I expel everything but Hill and me and this track.

I reach down and grab my handlebars. Hill grabs his handlebars. I catch a glance of Hill in my peripheral vision. *I'm going to fucking kill you*, I think.

We roll off the line. I lead. I creep along the bottom of the track, riding on the blue apron. As we approach the final lap, I move up to the top of the boards, baiting Hill to come underneath me. He takes the bait, but he goes too soon, not even waiting for the steep banking in the corner to increase his momentum. I jump straight onto his rear wheel. He's ramping up the speed and I'm tucked directly in his draft.

With 200 meters to go, I pull to the right of Hill. At 100 meters I'm beside him, and at the line I'm in the lead. I beat him by half a wheel.

After a 15-minute break between matches, we go to the start line again. The official blows the whistle. Hill leads. I creep up on him with a lap to go, riding high at the top of the track. Hill increases his pace, trying to fend me off. He rides in the center of the wide track, looking over his right shoulder. I ramp up my speed behind him, riding faster, faster, faster. He's looking over his right shoulder. I'm not there. I dive into the sliver of space Hill left open at the bottom of the track. We're elbow to elbow, exiting the second turn.

Three hundred meters to the finish, and I'm at full gas. Once the sprint starts, everything happens in a flash, like a film on fast-forward. We bump and jostle each other as we race down the back straight, but the physical exchanges are so rapid, I barely notice we've touched. I sprint with all my might, trying to break him. Finally, I fend Hill off. The race is mine to win, and mine to lose.

I bear down on the pedals. I sprint harder than anytime in my life. I'm sprinting for my life. I'm fighting off an attacking boar. Images of Christi and my unborn child flash through my head. I'm sprinting to become number one.

Hill makes his way back to my rear wheel as we enter the third turn. He swings wide up the banking and dives back down, gaining speed and pulling right beside me as we exit the final turn. I see the line. I throw my bike.

I'm world champion.

• • • • • • • • •

A wave of jubilation washes over me. *"Campione del mondo!"* The announcer shouts. I pump my fist in the air. I finish my cooldown lap, jump off my bike, and bear-hug Andrzej. I get down on my hands and knees and kiss the finish line. Camera flashes pop. I'm 23, and I'm the fastest cyclist in the world.

At the awards ceremony, Hill, Hübner, and I walk to the podium. I take the top step. I'm presented the rainbow jersey, bearing the colored stripes that signify a world champion. The national anthem crackles on over the loudspeakers. I stand solemnly, proud to represent the United States, to be an American. I try to hold in the wide grin that wants to spread across my face.

This is the happiest day of my life.

When I get back to the hotel room I'm sharing with Erv, some good-natured teasing ensues. He regained his place among the world's best kilo riders, nabbing a silver medal behind the Frenchman Florian Rousseau and ahead of the Australian he trained alongside in December, Shane Kelly. After his own awards ceremony, Erv came back to the room and slammed his medal down on the table.

"Beat that!" he told me.

Now it's my turn to taunt him. I gingerly lay my jersey over a chair.

"Don't sit here, Erv," I chide. "This seat belongs to the world champion-ship jersey."

Erv laughs. He couldn't be happier for me, and I for him. We did it. We met as kids, dreaming of being the best one day. Now we're men who've encouraged and pushed each other year after year. Now we're among the best ever in our disciplines.

· · · · · · · · ·

But I'm not done yet. After a rest day, the qualifying rounds for the keirin start.

I call Gil before the race. I tell him I'm going to lead out the sprint, again. He says it's risky. Hübner will patiently wait behind me, timing his sprint perfectly to beat me at the line. But I'm the strongest sprinter at these world championships. Gil agrees I should seize my own fate rather than fight in the keirin scrum.

We line up for the keirin finals and Andrzej holds me on the line. Andrzej and Gil are the only people I trust to hold me. They're my cor-ner men. They understand the technical aspects of the job, like how to set my foot in the proper start position, as well as the mental. Andrzej knows when to remind me of what I need to do during the race, and when to shut up and let me focus.

The starter's gun fires and I shoot off the line, grabbing first posi-tion behind the motorized pace bike. Hübner glues himself to my rear wheel. With a lap and a half to go on the long Palermo track, the pace bike pulls off. Six hundred meters remain. I put my head down and gradually wind up my sprint.

I start at 95 percent of my max speed. Every 100 meters I increase the pace. At 500 meters I'm at 97 percent. At 300 meters I'm at 98 per-cent. At 200 meters I'm going full speed. I'm in pain. My arms and legs start to seize with lactic acid as I push and pull on the handlebars and pedals with all the strength left in my body. The line can't come quickly enough. I feel Hübner behind me, leading the pack of racers.

One hundred meters. The swarm comes. I hear Hübner's strained breathing. From the corner of my eye, I see his contorted face beside me, inching closer and closer. I see the line . . . it's . . . right . . . there . . . I throw my bike, arms forward, head down.

"*Scheisse!*" Hübner yells as we cross the line.

. . . .

Back in the United States, Heinz has one of those feelings, as if something special happened. He is at the Boston Marathon working as a volunteer motorcycle official. But he slips into a phone booth and calls home to Trexlertown.

Mike rolls his wheelchair to the phone and picks up.

"Well, how did he do?" Heinz asks in his guttural German accent.

"He won, Dad," Mike says. "He won. The Blade is a double world champion."

After a few more minutes of conversation, Heinz hangs up the phone. It's brisk in Boston, and there's a cold wind whisking across Heinz's face, making his eyes water. That's the reason, he tells the other volunteers, that the tears are running down his cheeks.

. . . .

To put my world championships into historical context, you have to look way back to 1912, when the then-reigning king of American sprinting, Frank Kramer, won the match-sprint world championships. In front of tens of thousands of fans, on a now defunct wooden velodrome in Newark, New Jersey, Kramer beat the national champions of New Zealand and France to become the world's fastest bike racer.

Prior to his victory at worlds, Kramer had won the national championship every year since 1901. He was the highest-paid athlete in the United States, making double the salary of baseball's superstar, Ty Cobb. News of Kramer's world championship was a national sensation, covered in glowing detail by the *New York Times*.

Growing up in T-Town, I frequently listened to tales about Kramer. I scrutinized old black-and-white photos of Kramer, a thick man with a square, protruding jaw. He wore a red-and-white flag wrapped around his waist, signifying that he was America's best cyclist. I heard about how Kramer lost his first national championship to Major Taylor, but went on to dominate sprinting well into his forties. And how in his final race, before retiring, Kramer set a world record for a flying lap.

I dreamed of one day winning the world match-sprint title, just like Kramer. Now, my dream has come true. In the 82 years that passed between Kramer's world title and my own, no other American has won the match sprint at the world championships. And though I'm still no Frank Kramer, I do own a title he never held. I'm the first American to win a world title in the keirin since the event was introduced at the world championships in 1980.

I return to the Lehigh Valley anointed as a hometown hero. Hundreds of people gather at the Lehigh Valley International Airport to greet me. They erupt into cheers as I exit the plane. My mom and my dad are there. Gil jokingly grabs my rainbow-striped jersey and pulls it over his own head. Christi wraps her arms around me. I lift her off the ground and give her a big kiss. I rub her baby bump. Newspaper reporters clamor for quotes. Photographers snap photos of me standing beside my proud parents. I'm 23 years old. I soak in the attention.

A few days later, I'm invited to a ceremony at the county courthouse. The board of commissioners proclaims August 26 to be Marty Nothstein Day in Lehigh County. (Lest I lose my humility, I later find a $5 parking ticket on my car.)

Out of nowhere, I get a letter in the mail bearing the presidential seal. I open it and read the words of President Bill Clinton. "I commend you for the sportsmanship, discipline, and perseverance that earned you this great honor." At the bottom, the president's name is signed in black ink. I'm no Democrat, but my jaw still drops.

· · · · · · · · ·

At the final Friday night race of the year, the T-Town velodrome hosts an evening in celebration of my world championship wins. I decide to go for the flying-one-lap record. I obliterate the previous mark by over half a second. Then I end my season.

The sponsorship deals and salary contracts I dreamed of come to fruition. Christi and I talk about moving out of our cramped apartment and buying a home together. I enjoy my new status as number one, and I remain determined to keep it. I remain focused on winning Olympic gold.

I take my typical fall break, which includes plenty of peaceful time in the outdoors hunting, and then get back to work. By February, I'm deep into my preseason routine of exhausting road rides, debilitating gym workouts, and early bedtimes. Then, on the night of February 26 Christi rolls over in the bed and shoves me.

"What?" I moan.

"My water just broke," she says.

· · · · · · · · ·

A part of me doesn't realize the seriousness of what's happening. My child is preparing to emerge, and I'm thinking, it's early, I can still make my workout in the morning. A big snowstorm is coming, and I'm anxious to get to the gym before the roads shut down. But upon arriving at the hospital, I quickly understand the gravity of the situation.

As the evening progresses, Christi's contractions become more frequent, and more violent. It's well after midnight when the doctors tell Christi there's a problem. Her contraction won't release, and it's suffocating the baby. In a hurried moment of panic, a half dozen nurses rush into the room. They pull her out of the hospital bed and hold her up in the air. The doctors push on her stomach, trying to get the muscles to relax, but the contraction still won't release. So they start pushing even harder. I'm used to experiencing pain myself, but I can't bear to see her hurt.

Christi looks beyond the scrum of people and catches a glance of my face. She knows I'm impervious to nerves. I'm calm under pressure. I don't get scared. But when Christi sees my expression, she sees fear in my eyes for the first time. I fear we're going to lose this child—that I'm going to lose Christi.

Then, the contraction releases, and the doctors decide to perform an emergency C-section. One of the doctors recommends that I don't look, I might faint, but I tell him I'm accustomed to seeing blood. I watch as the doctors strap Christi down and slice open her stomach. They set her insides on a tray to one side of her, and pull the baby out from the other side.

Just as quickly as the panic started, it abates. Tyler Nothstein, 9 pounds, 4 ounces, enters the world. Christi and I had declined to find out the sex of the baby. (There aren't many actual surprises in life, let this be one, I'd said.) So when I discover it's a boy, I'm overjoyed. Though it might be politically incorrect to say so, I believe every man wants a son.

Once Christi is recovered from the surgery, Tyler is swaddled and placed in her arms. I sit beside her bed. The doctors and the nurses leave briefly. For a minute, it's just the three of us, Christi, Tyler, and me. We're a family. The feeling is a million times better than winning any bike race.

I was so wrong. *This* is the happiest day of my life.

. . . .

Though my home life is warm, the winter of 1995 is one of the cruelest in Lehigh Valley history for training. Months pass and the temperature rarely rises above freezing, even during the warmest part of the day. Snow comes down in droves.

My training routes remain wet, icy, and littered with salt even after the plows come through and pile the snow in towering banks along the curb. I'm trapped, training indoors for almost 100 consecutive days.

Of course, I could escape. I could go to San Diego, or Texas, or any assortment of warm locales where I could train under a bright sun instead of fluorescent lights. But I don't. I take pride in toughing out the miserable eastern Pennsylvania winters. The Lehigh Valley is my home. I want to remain with my family. I refused to risk missing the birth of my first child. My forebears overcame freezing sleet and howling northern winds to succeed, and so will I.

Thanks to Andrzej, I'm able to simulate my punishing track workouts inside. Upon joining the national team as the sprint coach, Andrzej commissioned the national team's go-to frame builder, Koichi Yamaguchi, to construct a machine we simply call, the Ergo. The name is short for Ergometer and the machine is a custom-made stationary bike dreamed up and designed by Andrzej.

Both Andrzej and Gil possess the minds of mechanical mad scientists. They're constantly trying to build a better mousetrap. They tinker with my race bike's hubs and bottom bracket until the bearings spin without an iota of resistance. But the Ergo is likely Andrzej's greatest creation.

To the unacquainted, the Ergo looks like a torture device. A 3-foot-wide base of thick steel tubes keeps the bike from swaying during all-out sprint efforts. Instead of running to the rear wheel, the Ergo's chain is attached to a flywheel at the front. To create resistance, Andrzej bolted wind-grabbing metal blades to the flywheel.

The Ergo's resistance is adjustable by moving the blades closer to, or farther away from, the flywheel. During the first iterations of the Ergo, the force of my pedaling sometimes throws the chain off the gears on the flywheel. The chain hits the metal blades and flings them across the room like throwing knives. Everyone ducks for cover. But over time, Andrzej dialed in the Ergo, even adding a rudimentary power meter made by the German company SRM that measures the watts I produce while pedaling. During workouts on the Ergo, I frequently max out at more than 2,300 watts.

By the winter of '95, I own three Ergos, all constructed by Yamaguchi to fit me exactly the same as my race bikes. One Ergo stays at the USA Cycling headquarters in Colorado Springs, one travels with me to major competitions, and one stays at my home in the Lehigh Valley. I spend hundreds of hours on the Ergo over the course of the 1995 winter, listening to heavy-metal music full blast and cranking out as many as a dozen full-tilt sprints during a training session.

The Ergo's flywheel makes a distinct, loud hum. When I work out with other national team members, the sound of multiple Ergos fills the room like a roaring jet engine. At the end of each interval, I always make sure my Ergo is the last one humming. Even though we're not moving, I need to feel as if I'm the strongest, as if I won, as if I'm number one.

· · · · · · · · ·

A week after Tyler is born, I fly to Mar del Plata, Argentina, for the Pan-Am Games, a qualifier for the Atlanta Olympics. The Pan-Ams are inexplicably held early in the year and serve as my first major test of the season. I'm told there are rumors among the national team members that I'm unprepared, that the birth of my son diverted my focus and the indomitable Lehigh Valley winter sapped my form. I pledge to prove the rumors wrong and secure my place on the Olympic team.

I sharpen my form with a week on the track in Argentina prior to the Pan Ams, then enter the match-sprint tournament. Before the qual-ifying time trial I grab a thick Sharpie and write "TYLER" on the wrists of my white leather gloves. I know exactly whom I'm riding for in Argentina—the newest member of my team.

The ideal conditions for riding a fast time trial deteriorate precipi-tously as I line up for my flying 200 meters. A fierce wind swirls around the velodrome and whips across the concrete track surface. I sprint down the back straight and through the final turn, battling gusts that catch my rear disc wheel and push me up the track's banking. I cross the line at 10.5 seconds, a new Pan-Am Games record.

I go on to dominate every round of the match-sprint tournament, winning the gold medal. I secure my spot for the Atlanta Olympics.

. . . .

On Labor Day, I'm sparring with another sprinter during a training camp, preparing for the '95 worlds. I whip my bike down the banking to start a sprint and the force of my pedaling causes the rear wheel of my bike to suddenly fold in half. I slam into the concrete and slide for 20 feet, my skin tearing away from my body, before I finally come to a stop.

Another crash. My third bad fall of the year. In May I suffered a concussion at a World Cup in Greece, and in August I dislocated my shoulder at track nationals. I lift myself up and begin to assess the dam-age. I look at my right knee. Just minutes after the crash, it's swollen to double the size of my left. "It's broken," I say.

"You broke your kneecap," my doctor, Thomas Meade, tells me. But you're lucky, he says. It's not cracked in half, only broken on the side. He says the long-term prognosis is good. I should recover in 4 to 6 weeks. I tell him I intend to race at worlds in 3 weeks. To compete at 100 per-cent, you'll need a miracle, Dr. Meade says.

He drains 80 ccs of blood from my knee and then puts the joint in a brace, immobilizing it. After a few days, the brace comes off, and Randi Neri makes magic happen, again. My knee heals more quickly than anyone could've imagined. Though I'm still nowhere near 100 percent, I'm riding 200-meter times close to national-record pace just a week before heading off to worlds.

I fly to Bogota, Colombia, for worlds and decide to focus on the team sprint, my best chance for a medal on the injured knee. I join forces with a fellow sprinter, Bill Clay, and Erv, the kilo specialist. All of us are among the best in the world at our individual events. We make it to the bronze-medal match, where we face Spain. Each of us will ride a lap at the front of our three-man group, then peel off the track. The Spanish team lines up on the opposite side of the track.

Clay starts us off, and it's a good start. We're two-tenths of a second up on the Spaniards after one lap. Then I take over, with Erv tightly tucked in my slipstream. At the end of my turn, we're ahead by a full half second. On the last lap, Erv goes to work. He settles into his aero bars and rips the final lap, adding another tenth of a second to our lead over Spain. We win the bronze. It's the only medal I will take home from the '95 world championships.

Fall is in full swing when I return to the Lehigh Valley. I spend my brief off-season hunting in the woods. I allow my knee to fully recover. Then, I get back to work. Fewer than 300 days remain until the Atlanta Olympics. I know I'll be ready. I'm certain I'll win.

Above: Wheels were always part of my life—bikes, motorcycles, go-Karts, cars, and trucks. My father, Wayne, owned Ford and Dodge dealerships as well as ran the family trucking company with his brother. That's me as a toddler, my dad, and brother Tim in the dune buggy.

Right: Growing up, I was taken by anything competitive. My fighting spirit made me good at sports: football, baseball, basketball, wresting, BMX, and even throwing rocks. I won a couple of home run derbies when I played Little League baseball for the East Penn Youth Association. I'd swing the bat as if I was trying to decapitate someone.

Photographs courtesy of the Nothstein family

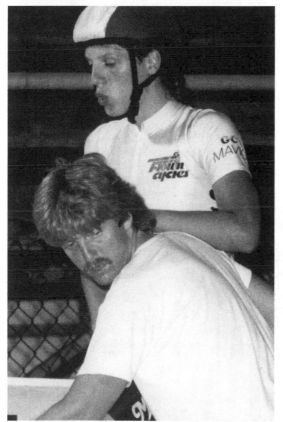

Above, left: Me and my brother Jay (*rear*) and our friend Chris Roberts (*left*) started weight lifting to shape up for sports in middle school. As you can see, we were huge!

Above, right: I started riding competitively as part of the Air Products Development program in 1986 and won my first medals. I was hooked. I remember riding so much I wore out my cycling clothes that first year.

Left: Later, I was helped by guys like Mark Whitehead (shown with me here in 1988). Whitehead, nicknamed the Outlaw, was a pro racer who I used to watch ride at T-Town even before I started racing.

Photographs courtesy of the Nothstein family

Above: Robert "Bob" Rodale fires the starting gun one evening at the Trexlertown, PA, velodrome in this archive photo from the 1970s. The late CEO of Rodale Inc., publisher of this book, always had a fondness for bicycling and he envisioned a velodrome in the Lehigh Valley for recreational and competitive cycling. In 1974, he donated 25 acres of farmland and oversaw construction of a park that would contain the nation's premier bike-racing track. (*Photographs courtesy of Rodale Inc.*)

Below: Here's a view of the Valley Preferred Cycling Center, of which I am executive director, as it looks today. This is the same track on which I first learned to ride a track bike and cut my teeth in racing.

Above: I owe much of my racing success to the coaxing, pushing, and strategizing of my "team": (*from left to right*) my soigneur Eddie Balcerzak, and coaches Gil "Gibby" Hatton (in cap) and Andrzej Bek.

Right: Gil, "the man behind the man," gives me a push onto the track at the 1996 Olympic Games in Atlanta.

Photographs courtesy of Marty Nothstein

Above: "*Campione del mondo!*" I'm 23 and I'm the fastest cyclist in the world. I wear the rainbow jersey signifying a world champion, having defeated the Australian sprinter Darryn Hill (*left*) and German Michael Hübner (*right*) in Palermo, Italy, in 1994. (*Photograph courtesy of the Nothstein family*)

Below: This is a nice whitetail buck I shot on a hunting trip in Montana. I've loved the outdoors and hunting all my life. I've been a bowhunter since I was 11 years old. In fact, I lied about my age just to get my license a year early. (*Photograph courtesy of Macon Cherp*)

Above: I am an Olympic champion finally. Here, I'm celebrating with some of my family—from *left*, my mother Gail, daughter Devon, wife Christi, and son Tyler. *(Photograph courtesy of Mike Powell/Getty Images Sport)*

Below: Match sprint is an intimate event—the riders nudge, jostle, even headbutt for position. Here, Jens Fiedler, the German Olympic and world champion sprinter, and I battle for the lead in the final round of the World Cup in British Columbia. *(Photograph courtesy of Casey B. Gibson)*

Above: Train, eat, sleep… dream about the Olympics. That was my life. But it was all worth it for the life that cycling has given to me and my family, culminating in a special final moment on the track in Australia with my son. "Look at all the people!" I tell Tyler on our victory lap. *(Photograph courtesy of Cox Enterprises)*

Part 2

8
THE DEMONS OF ATLANTA

I DIDN'T go to Atlanta for the silver.

I get home and am single-minded about getting back on track, back to number one. I immediately start preparing for the 1996 world championships in England. At worlds I hope to get my rematch with Fiedler. The directors of the T-Town velodrome invited Fiedler to come race me here, at home, after the Olympics. But he declined.

So instead of racing Fiedler on a Friday night at T-town, 2 weeks before worlds, I reluctantly agree to race the tandem with Nick Chenowth. Nick is my boss. He's a masters racer who also manages EDS, the multimillion-dollar team I ride for.

I'm no tandem-racing rookie. But after too many close calls—and after seeing a competitor nearly die while riding against Erv and me at the Olympic Trials in '92—I swore off tandems.

It's not just me, either. Because of the danger, tandem racing fell out of favor internationally during the '90s, and is no longer an Olympic or world championship event. T-Town is the only track in the States that still sanctions the discipline. Every August the track turns a normal Friday night into Tandemonium. The event doubles as the tandem national championships, and Nick is keen on winning a title with me as his driver. Nick lives to race tandems. Even though I know the risks of tandem racing, Nick signs my checks, so I agree to do it.

In the first sprint of our first-round match, I'm piloting the tandem to a win down the track's back straight.

As the banking steepens in the third turn, I feel the tire go soft. "Easy, easy, easy," I shout back to Nick. Then I hear the tire explode. It's the sound of a shotgun during dove season, a car backfiring, a balloon exploding. *Boom!* The rear tire of the tandem disintegrates, peeling off of the wheel. The 6-foot-long carbon-fiber bike fishtails beneath our combined 400 pounds of body weight.

Don't tense up, Nick. Don't tense up, I think.

But he does. He tries to correct us, and his movement on the back of the bike sends us further out of control. I feel the back of the bike sliding up the track, so I countersteer into the banking—just as Nick leans left. With a violent thud, we topple over. My helmet cracks as my head smacks against the concrete track. I hemorrhage skin from the entire left side of my body. As we skid back down the banking toward the apron, I leave behind a trail of blood and tissue on the light gray track surface.

The audience ringing the track gasps. People cover their mouths in horror.

Finally, we stop sliding. I begin to regain clarity. A huddle of coaches, officials, and medical personnel gather around me. They unstrap my feet from the pedals and pull the tandem off me. This is my third tire blowout with Nick, and my second hard crash.

Skip Cutting, an EDS coach and former three-time Olympian, walks into the medical room where I'm assessing my skin loss. Since our tire blew out in the first round, the officials offer us a reride. "The bike's ready to go," Skip says.

"Fuck that," I tell him. "I'm never getting on that thing again."

But I'm not done competing. A full schedule of racing remains on the evening's schedule, and the stands are packed with fans, most of them here to welcome me home after the Olympics. I won't let them down. After I finish dressing my wounds, I grab my silver GT track bike and a new helmet. I hobble over the top rail of the track, and the crowd collectively quiets. *Unbelievable. He's back.* I race nearly everything remaining on the evening's schedule, from the points race to the sprints. I win all my heats in the sprint tournament and the final, then I'm off to worlds.

· · · · · · · · ·

A week after my crash, Andrzej, Gil, and I arrive in Manchester, England, for worlds. I'm stiff and sore. My wounds ooze and stick to the sheets at night. My left knee throbs and clicks when I bend it. After a round of 500-meter sprints on Tuesday, my brain started pounding. Those headaches, they should subside, the doctors tell me.

Not only am I physically banged up heading into the race, I'm mentally scarred, too. The Olympics gnaw at me every day. I lost gold. I think about the Atlanta Olympics a thousand times per day. The loss haunts me in my sleep. *I will redeem myself at worlds.*

Andrzej knows the dangers of tandem racing well. I've rubbed the dent in Andrzej's skull from his own horrific tandem crash. But he's not upset I raced nationals with Nick. "You must accept sprinting is dangerous. There is no place for fear," he tells me.

Luckily Andrzej brought along my favorite soigneur, Eddie Balcerzak, to work out my aches and pains. A good soigneur means as much to my team as a coach or mechanic, and Eddie is one of the best. I tried out a couple of guys between Eddie and my previous great soigneur, Waldek Stepniowski, but none of them worked out. Then Andrzej introduced me to Eddie, a fellow Pole, and we clicked. He understands cycling, and he understands me.

In the '80s, Eddie raced professionally and coached a top cycling club in Warsaw. He came to the United States in '85 and worked for

7-Eleven, the first American pro team to ride the Tour de France. Now he's helping me attempt to win another world championship.

Eddie's massages are the best part of my day. I feel as if I'm getting worked over with a meat tenderizer. He's built like a bull, thick and round with massive shoulders. The fingers on his hands look like Polish sausages but are composed entirely of muscle. He pummels the knots in my thighs as if they insulted his mother. We don't talk when I'm on the massage table. I just lie there and enjoy the good hurt.

In the downtime between training sessions at the Manchester velodrome, I keep things light by messing with Eddie. One day while he's taking a nap, Gil and I sneak into his room and turn the heat all the way up. Sweat starts beading on Eddie's forehead and dark stains appear in his pits. I stifle my laugh in the next room. "NOTE-STINE!" Eddie bellows when he finally wakes up, a wet mess, and figures out what the hell is going on. He jumps out of bed and starts chasing me. I scamper down the hall before he can grab me. If Eddie gets a hand on you, you're dead.

On Wednesday, we stop messing around and get to work. The Manchester track is the jewel of British cycling. Just 2 years old, the sleek, modern-looking building houses an indoor 250-meter wooden velodrome, as well as the offices for the UK's national cycling federation. The track has a reputation for insanely fast times.

My first event is the keirin. To make the finals, I must place at the front end of two qualifying rounds. In the first qualifying round, I ride as if I just lost Olympic gold. I'm pissed. I punish my opponents and easily qualify for the semifinal. In the semis, I meet Fiedler.

But Fiedler owns two Olympic gold medals. He's not concerned with a rematch. He rides as if he doesn't care about another world championship medal, too. In the closing laps of our race, he leans his shoulder into an opponent whose spot in line he wants, and gives him a headbutt with that little white cap. Fiedler finishes in the top three and qualifies for the finals, but the officials disqualify him.

I move on to the medal race. Fiedler goes home.

· · · · · · · · ·

The lineup for the finals reads like an all-star roster of keirin racers: There's the defending world champ, France's Frédéric Magné, and his teammate, Laurent Gané, a pair that will work together to beat me; the 1993 keirin world champion, Australian Gary Neiwand, who desperately wants his title back; a feisty wild card, Pavel Buran from the Czech Republic; and the giant from Germany, Michael Hübner. Hübner owns three keirin world titles—the most of all time. I won the world title in the keirin in '94. I want one more.

We line up. I plan to race the keirin just as I race the match sprint. I want the early lead. Of course, everyone else will too. The first sprint comes off the start line. The official blows his whistle. The motorbike takes off. Andrzej shoves me as if he's pushing a piano up a flight of stairs. My single giant gear is made for sprinting from a full gallop, not a dead stop. I hump my bike, throwing my weight forward and in front of the pedals. Neiwand's next to me, doing the same. I stomp on the pedals and surge ahead of the group. I slip in as first wheel behind the motorbike, and Neiwand takes the position behind me.

The laps tick by. Warm fumes from the motorbike's exhaust blow across my shins. I look back over my left shoulder. Buran sits behind Neiwand, then Magné, Hübner, and Gané. Andrzej and I develop two game plans before every keirin, depending on the opponents and my position behind the motorbike. Because I captured the lead off the start line, I don't need to worry about getting to the front once the motorbike pulls off the track and the real racing starts. I will defend my position at the front until the last lap, then I'll unleash my full sprint. I figure Hübner and Magné will make an early charge to the front. The big German, Hübner, is a drag racer, like me. He'll want a long sprint. Magné is a tactician. If I make any mistakes, he'll capitalize.

The motorbike gradually picks up speed as the finish approaches. Five laps to go. Four. Three. Twenty-five miles per hour. Twenty-eight.

Thirty. The motorbike accelerates and peels off the track. Race on. Neiwand jumps out of the saddle. I feel him moving up on my left. But I won't let anyone pass without a fight. I start my own charge to hold him off. Then Magné makes his move over the top of the group as expected. Hübner follows, tight on Magné's wheel.

Two laps to go. I hold Magné at my shoulder through the first turn. He's the crest of a wave of racers. Behind him is the white water. If I get trapped back there, I'll wash right out of this race. Magné pulls in front of me on the back straight and through the third turn. I grab his rear wheel. I ride the crest of the wave, in front of the white water. Then, inexplicably, Magné slows. He tries to force someone else to the front before the last lap sprint. But we're going damn near 40 miles per hour now. No time to hit the breaks.

The white water starts to envelop me. Neiwand slides up on my inside and Gané sprints from the back, inching up on my left. I whip my bike, first down the banking to fend off Neiwand, then to my right stalling Gané. The bell rings. One lap to go. Magné leads. I'm right behind him. One rider separates me from another keirin world title.

Magné leaps out of the saddle. We fly through the first turn. I draw beside him on the back straight. Gané makes another charge on my right. I'm in a French sprinter sandwich. We round the final turn and I beat back Gané with a hook up the banking. We exit the final turn and I'm even with Magné. I unleash my six hardest pedal strokes over the last 50 meters. I fly past Magné. Neiwand makes a late charge on my inside. He throws his bike—but he's too late. I'm world keirin champ.

Gil stands on the track apron as I spin past. He pumps his fist high in the air.

· · · · · · · · ·

We get one day to rest before the match-sprint tournament starts. My body's a mess. I lie in bed with a giant bag of ice on my left knee and give the requisite interviews to local papers and cycling publications back in the United States. *Something's not right with it,* I can tell.

"Just one more event," Gil and Andrzej tell me. If I win the match sprint, I'm double world champion for the second time in my career.

On day one of the match-sprint tournament, I tell myself I just need to sprint four times. Once each in the first and second rounds, which are single elimination, and two more times in the best-of-three, quarter-final match. I win my first-round and second-round races riding away from my opponents. Then, in the quarters, I meet the Czech, Buran. He finished sixth in the Olympic match sprint just a month earlier.

I beat Buran outright in the first sprint. One more sprint and I'm done for the day. I can go ice my knee and dream about winning a gold medal tomorrow. But Buran fights me in the second sprint. He makes a good run on me along the back straight, so I throw him a nasty hook. Only, Buran doesn't react as quickly as I think he will. I knock his front wheel out from under him and put him on the ground. Amazingly, instead of disqualifying me, the officials order a reride. Buran gets up. We sprint again.

This time he tries to pass me in the final turn. I hook him again but obviously come out of the sprinter's lane. I'm relegated. The officials give Buran the win. The winner of the next ride wins the round and will race for medals tomorrow.

My left knee throbs. *One more sprint.*

The three previous sprints, and the crash, catch up with Buran on the final ride. I win cleanly and move on to the semifinals. That evening Eddie rubs my legs. I ice my knee. The patella is thick and red. The joint creaks when I bend my leg. Tendonitis, Eddie says. Something's not right.

I'm paired against Darryn Hill in the semis. Hill smells blood when we line up. He's a shark. A killer, like me. I lead off the line. Hill stalks me. With a lap and a half to go he comes through underneath me and whips his back wheel across the front of my bike. Intimidation. I'm not scared.

We start the sprint with a lap to go. He's flying. I can't get past him in the final turn. He wins easily and throws his hand up in the air as if he won the round. Every part of me wants to jump off my bike and beat him into the ground, but I just spin past him.

"Put your arm down, you fucking stink," I say.

"Fuck you," he barks back.

We line up for the second sprint. Despite his bluster, Hill looks tired. I'm going to make this sprint long, I decide. Let's see how he holds that top-end speed. Hill leads off the line. I start ramping up my sprint with two laps to go. He's determined not to let me pass, and matches my pace from the front. Every time he looks back I'm coming faster, faster. Hill puts his head down and pedals harder. By the time we hit the line for one lap to go, we're near an all-out sprint. Hill can't hold me off anymore.

I charge directly at his rear wheel in the first turn. If Hill tries to hook me high, I'll come underneath. If he guards the inside, I'll sprint over the top. Hill lowers his head and looks under his left armpit. I'm a red-white-and-blue behemoth bearing down on his right side. As I draw near, Hill moves up the banking. I dive for his inside just as he whips the rear end of his bike. His back wheel moves like the tail of a snake. Inches separate my front tire from his rear wheel as it flicks down the track. I immediately adjust and steer back to his right, but now Hill's rear wheel is moving in the opposite direction. The wheel zings up the track's banking. I back off my pedals and lean to my right, just in time to avoid a collision.

We keep sprinting down the back straight. Hill beats me to the finish. The officials review the tape. I head back to the national team's cabin to warm down. I know this isn't over. I see Hill in the Australian cabin. He's lying down. His stomach is still heaving. He's out of shape. "Get up, you fat fuck," I tell him. "We're not done yet."

Eventually, the officials decide Hill cheated. They relegate him and give me the win. Win one more sprint and I make the gold-medal match. Before our final match, Hill and I are called to the waiting area near the start line and seated in a row of four chairs—we sit with two empty chairs between us. We don't talk or look at each other.

Then we line up for the final sprint. I lead. We round the turn coming into one lap to go. Hill ramps up his speed. I see him coming and start to kick. I keep him at my hip through the first turn and down the back straight. We enter the turn toward the finish and Hill fades.

I cross the line, uncontested. But I've wasted valuable energy locking antlers with Hill. I should have put him away earlier.

· · · · · · · · ·

Except for me, the top four match sprinters from the Olympics skipped the world championship tournament. The Canadian, Harnett, didn't show at all. Neiwand took his keirin silver back to Australia. Fiedler's already back in Germany.

I don't blame any of them for not showing. I'm almost done, too. Two more sprints I tell myself. Two more sprints and my season ends. Two more sprints on my swollen knee. Win two more sprints, and I win worlds.

In the finals I meet Florian Rousseau—the man who beat Erv for Olympic gold in the kilo. He's calm, quiet—a silent assassin. He likes long sprints, but he's quick too. The National Institute for Sport, a school in France that churns out Olympic athletes, trained Rousseau well. He's 22 and already owns four world titles.

On the start line Rousseau bulges out his eyes and bares his teeth before grabbing the handlebars. He doesn't appear to know, or even care, if I'm on the track. He leads off the line. Unlike Fiedler, Rousseau doesn't try to keep me from reaching my top speed. He's a kilo rider. He bets his top speed is faster than mine, and that he can hold it longer.

We wind up our gears with a little more than a lap to go. Rousseau leads out the sprint, daring me to get past him. He doesn't swerve, or try to disrupt my momentum. We just put our heads down and sprint to the line, side by side. I'm at his shoulder exiting the final turn, but I can't get any closer. He wins by half a wheel, and hardly looks winded.

In the second ride I don't even get past Rousseau's rear wheel. He's going too fast and I'm out of gas. He wins the world championships. I lose. After Atlanta, after the tandem crash, after the keirin win, and after all the early-round sprints on a jacked knee, I'm out of gas. It's time to go home to the Lehigh Valley, and rest.

I've had the best season of my career. I finish 1996 the number one–ranked track sprinter in the world. But despite the success, I can't escape the thought of losing gold.

9

WORLD CUP, CALI, COLUMBIA

WHEN I get home from Manchester, I go see Dr. Meade at Allentown Sports Medicine. Meade knows me and my injuries well by this point. He's also one of the nation's top sports orthopedists. He's worked with pro ball players from the Phillies and the Eagles, but says nothing trumps teaming up with an Olympian. His own competitive feats include qualifying for an Ironman triathlon during his medical residency and setting world records as part of a masters swimming club. He intimately understands my mind-set. He knows what it means to push the body to its physical limits—to the point where it breaks down.

An MRI ordered by Dr. Meade confirms my suspicions: something's not right. He points to a split in the meniscus, the squishy cartilage cushioning the joint, and says that this is the source of my pain. I likely ripped the cartilage when I crashed with Nick on the tandem. Dr. Meade says he can fix the meniscus arthroscopically, by sticking a small camera and other surgical instruments into my knee capsule. He also says that if he sees more damage inside the knee than just the meniscal tear, he'll need to perform an open surgery, slicing the knee wide open.

The recovery from the tiny incision required for an arthroscopic procedure pales in comparison to the recovery from an open surgery. Athletes often return to training a week or so after getting scoped. Dr. Meade says an open surgery may need up to 3 months to heal.

I don't want surgery at all. I've seen too many athletes go under the knife and never return to their previous form. But if I must get surgery, I want the scope, and a quicker return to top form. After my medal performance in Atlanta, I stand to make thousands of dollars in bonuses from every race I win.

But Meade doesn't make any promises. "I'll do what's right for the knee in the long run," he says. If he sees damage that he can't repair arthroscopically, he won't hesitate to slice me open. The Sydney Olympics are 4 years away, Meade reminds me.

That October, I go under. Meade calls working on me his own orthopedic Olympics. The pressure's immense. If he flubs a diagnosis or makes an erroneous cut, my career may end and possibly his, too. My meniscal tear sits at the front of the knee; this is different from nearly 90 percent of meniscal tears, which occur at the back of the knee capsule. In the tandem crash, I likely hyperextended my knee, clipping the meniscus at the front.

Meade trims the cartilage around the tear, making it smooth so it won't catch on the joint and cause irritation. But the frontal meniscal tear causes a second problem—one that a simple scope can't fix. The tear allowed joint fluid to sneak out from the knee capsule and form a grapelike cyst behind my patellar tendon. Meade decides to open up the knee and take out the cyst. If he doesn't, it will continue to grow, thickening beneath the patella tendon and causing chronic knee pain.

The moment Meade makes a 4-inch slice down the middle of my knee, I'm looking at 3 months of recovery, instead of 3 weeks. But Meade's determined to do what's right for my knee. The cyst looks like a small grape, but with a neck like a water balloon. He saws off the neck of the cyst, so it won't come back. Because he's got my knee open, he also adds a couple stitches to strengthen the meniscal repair.

Meade says the pain in my patella isn't tendonitis, which corresponds to an inflammatory issue, but tendinosis—microtears running longitudinally along the tendon. He makes an elliptical incision in the patella and removes a dead and withered piece of the tendon tissue. Meade theorizes the added trauma will increase blood flow to the tendon, aiding its recovery as the rest of the knee heals.

When I wake up, Meade tells me that, other than the meniscal tear, cyst, and patella tendinosis, my knee is in great condition. I should recover just fine, he says.

· · · · · · · · ·

Turns out, the surgery and subsequent extended recovery are exactly the forced break I need. My body demands rest and my mind wants time away from bike racing. The disappointment of silver in Atlanta continues to haunt me, every day.

Fall in the Lehigh Valley is my favorite season. The wind blows across the valley floor with a brisk, refreshing bite. The hills turn bright amber and red. It's archery season for deer hunting. My left knee is immobilized by a bulky brace and I'm bound to a pair of crutches, but I've never missed deer season and I won't start now. For me, there is no better therapy, physical or mental.

I grab my bow and convince Gil to drive me into the woods. I spot a large tree with big stable branches—the perfect stand. Gil helps me as I clamber up into the tree with my one good leg. I pull an arrow from the quiver. The fall breeze flicks the leaves off the trees. They flutter to the ground like colored snowflakes sifting through a kaleidoscope. I wait in silence for the soft crackling of hooves on the bed of leaves below.

For those few hours in the woods, bow in hand, I forget about Atlanta and losing gold. I find solace. I feel restored.

· · · · · · · · ·

I spend the winter recovering in the home I built before the Olympics. The house sits on 22 acres in the hills north of T-Town. Though I didn't win gold in Atlanta, the house gives me an amazing sense of accomplishment. I've provided a home for my family. I've also begun reclaiming the land of my ancestors, the original settlers of Pennsylvania. Land is the greatest treasure a PA Dutchman can own.

In December, Christi and I get married. It's a small wedding at our new home with a few dozen close friends and family. I realize December isn't the ideal time for a wedding in the Northeast, but again, my training and racing comes first. Christi understands. She always does. A spring wedding would never work with my racing schedule.

The surgery made me anxious. Ready to get back to work. The season's first World Cup is in Cali, Colombia, this May. I'm likely to see Fiedler in the match sprint there. Gil and I aggressively rehab my knee. Typically I focus on heavy free weights late in the winter, but the surgery left my quad atrophied and weak.

Instead I work with lighter weights, doing multiple reps. I perform one-legged lifts on machines to isolate and balance my muscle groups. I do what I can to continue getting stronger and faster without hurting my healing knee. I murder my upper body with biceps curls and incline presses.

When I'm healthy enough to start riding, I go to the Olympic Training Center in Chula Vista, California, for a six-week training camp.

The first racing on my repaired knee comes in February. Andrzej and I accept an invitation to a European six-day in Milan. Six-day races date back to the golden era of track racing in the US. From the late 1800s to the middle of the 20th century, tens of thousands of fans flocked to six-days held in Manhattan at Madison Square Garden.

The events initially required racers to compete around the clock for six days straight. Whoever completed the most laps, won. Promoters purposely marketed the inhumanity of the six-day races to attract press coverage and spectators. In 1896, the 18-year-old Major Taylor churned out 1,732 miles at a six-day in Madison Square Garden, the equivalent of riding from New York to Houston. After New York State passed a law forbidding competitors from racing for more than 12 straight hours, promoters adopted a two-person, relay-style format—which today is known as the Madison.

When track racing died out in the US at the end of the 1930s, the six-day scene moved to Europe—where it's still insanely popular. The two-man team format remains the basis of the modern, European six-day circuit.

In Milan, the promoters install a portable velodrome at the Forum sports palace, and transform the infield of the velodrome into a fine restaurant. Formally dressed spectators sip champagne and dine at rows of tables dressed with white tablecloths, as the racers fly past on the track encircling the restaurant. The rowdiest fans occupy the bleachers, drinking and smoking and cheering late into the evening. By the time the races finally wrap up, well past midnight, there is a haze of cigarette smoke collected beneath the velodrome ceiling.

I thrive on the festive atmosphere at six-day races. The scene rivals any in professional sports. It's the closest I ever come to feeling like a rock star performing in a packed arena. Fans gather outside our hotels, and hound us for autographs. Spreads of gourmet Italian food await us after we compete. At one immaculately prepared buffet, mozzarella is presented as balls of white cheese floating in water, instead of baked on top of a greasy pizza. "What are these?" I ask Andrzej. He looks at me as if I'm an ingrate.

Because the European six-days center on endurance events, the sprinters act as a sideshow. We come onto the track for brief performances twice a night—while the main attraction, the two-man teams, take a break. The sprinters race flying-200-meter time trials, followed by a short sprint tournament. The crowd delights in the size, speed, and power of the sprinters. We strut out onto the velodrome like the lions at the circus.

Despite our frequently late bedtimes, Andrzej insists I train through the Milan six-day. He rouses me from bed every day at 7 a.m. for early training sessions on the track while the rest of the sprinters sleep in. Initially, my knee holds up to the racing. But by the third day, it's aching constantly. Worst of all, I can't find a bag of ice anywhere in Milan. I start counting down each individual sprint I'll need to perform before I go home.

My primary competitors throughout the week include some of the top Italian and French riders. I race Roberto Chiappa and Federico Paris, Italians who frequently sit atop World Cup podiums, as well as the French keirin specialist, Magné. I don't come anywhere near my best flying-200 times, but I still easily win the tournament. I'm officially honored as the top overall sprinter in Milan, but I still need time to let my knee regain its full strength.

· · · · · · · · ·

Three months later, I fly to Colombia, where I anticipate a rematch with Fiedler. As always on the flight to an event, I sit next to Erv. Typically Erv is calm and relaxed, a perfectly serene being heading into major competitions. But now he's freaking out.

Erv harbors a fear of flying so deep it affects him physically. Just over a year before our trip, a large commercial airplane crashed into the steep mountains surrounding Cali, and as our own flight approaches the airport we see flashes of lightning out the plane's windows. The plane bounces violently in the turbulence. The captain orders the flight attendants to sit down and buckle up. Overhead bins jar open and luggage spills out.

Another sprinter, Bill Clay, peeks out the window. "Wow, check out how cool the lightning looks," he says, having no idea Erv is turning into a stinking pile of sweat next to me. Erv leans over me, toward the window. "What do you see out there?" he asks. A lightning strike brightens the night sky, and we catch a glimpse of the jagged mountaintops. Thunder cracks. The plane rocks. Erv gulps. Now he's made me nervous.

We land safely; the real peril is on the ground. Throughout the '90s, Colombia is often cited as one of the world's most dangerous places. The cocaine trade and bloody battles between competing cartels ravage the country. The drug violence accounts for more than 30,000 murders. Cali serves as ground zero for this vicious drug war. Law enforcement officials refer to the local drug lords, the Cali Cartel, as the world's most powerful criminal organization. The cartel controls a militia known as Los Rastrojos, a ruthless gang of more than 1,000 hit men.

Fearing for our safety, the US Olympic Committee sends security forces with us to the World Cup—undercover guys in black suits, carrying handguns. Team officials instruct us not to wear any clothing bearing the USA logo outside of competition. When we arrive at the Cali airport, the local government provides us with a half dozen Colombian security forces, as well—teenagers in camouflage holding submachine guns.

On the way to the hotel, a couple of the fatigue-clad kids ride on our bus, while the other four drive ahead of us on two little dirt bikes. One kid drives while another sits backward on the bike, an automatic rifle across his thighs. Though they look threatening, I doubt these pubescent Colombian security guards would offer much defense should the Cali Cartel decide to take the team hostage. I imagine grabbing the machine gun myself and providing our own protection if we come under attack.

Besides the threat of sudden death, Cali generally isn't a pleasant place to visit. It's hot and humid. Our hotel stinks. But in part due to the lackluster accommodations and undeniable sense of danger, I love racing in Cali. The third-world conditions cause other athletes to bitch and moan, but I brush it off. Control what you can control, I say. The air of danger charges me up. I always kick major ass here.

The wooden track suits me perfectly. It's long and oval, shaped like a cigar with tight turns and long straights. The corners require deft handling skills while the straights favor a big top-end speed like mine. I fake out opponents in the turns and blow by them in the straightaways.

South Americans take their sports passionately, and these Colombians love cycling. The scene is like no other bike race on earth. The locals come out in droves to watch, spilling into the aisles. They whistle, bang drums, and chant in Spanish. The noise swirls around the velodrome, flowing out the sides of the open-air track and reverberating off the canopy ceiling above. The Colombians tailgate in the hills surrounding the track, and I can see the flickering of their campfires off in the distance. The smell of barbecued chicken wafts through the velodrome. Beautiful Colombian women, wearing next to nothing, saunter around the bleachers.

My knee isn't 100 percent yet, but the pain is bearable at this point. I'm confident heading into the match sprint, and qualify third in the flying-200-meter time trial. I breeze through the opening rounds, and run into Fiedler in the quarterfinals.

Before my match with Fiedler, a thunderstorm rolls in just as the sun dips behind the giant mountains ringing the city. The hot, muggy air cools suddenly, and lightning flashes in the distance. Rain crashes down, rolling off the open ends of the velodrome ceiling like giant window blinds of flowing water.

I take a deep breath. The musty storm air fills my lungs. The crowd's really going now—whistling, chanting, beating those drums. *Louder. C'mon, chant louder,* I think. Fiedler and I line up. I will exact my revenge right now. I will prove I'm number one.

Fiedler glares at me. I know he wants the same. We roll off the line. Fiedler leads. The drums beat as I flick my bike back and forth behind him. The bell signaling the last lap rings. I charge Fiedler. I slingshot through the first turn and hit top speed on the long back straight, flying past him. He doesn't give up, but he's not even close. There's no photo finish this time around. The drums beat louder.

I lead the second sprint, and Fiedler gives more fight, but can't get any closer than the rear axle of my bike as we cross the line. I beat Fiedler. I get a semblance of revenge. In the final I beat a French prodigy named Arnaud Tournant.

I line up for the keirin finals as the undisputed favorite, the guy everyone is gunning for. The race is fast and aggressive. I take a risk and wait to make my move on the final lap. As the track banking transitions to the finishing straight, I come over the top of two other riders and I power across the line first.

I'm invincible. I've got my swagger back. I head back to T-Town with two gold medals from international competition.

But neither of them are Olympic gold.

10

SACRIFICE

AS THE '97 season progresses, my knee feels better and better. I should get faster and faster. But after the double-gold-medal performance in Cali, my results fluctuate. A World Cup comes to T-Town for the first time ever. The local media heralds me as the hometown favorite. But I finish second in both the match sprint and the keirin, losing to Hill twice in close races. At a World Cup in Italy, I win the keirin but lose to two lesser-known Latvian riders in the match sprint. In Australia, I win another keirin. I started the year dominantly, but I've also shown that, at times, I'm beatable.

The losses don't bother me, though, not like Atlanta. I couldn't care less about any race, except the next Olympics—whether it's a local race at T-Town, a national-level event, or the world championships. It's not that I race with any less intensity. When my wheel hits the start line, I aim to cross the finish first, every time.

I don't dominate every race I enter because, physically, I'm tired. As my knee heals, I'm able to train harder and harder with less and less rest. Training is the only way I know of to fight the demons of my loss in Atlanta. I train nonstop. If I'm quicker and more powerful, I will not lose in Sydney.

Like most top-level athletes, I train in blocks. Block training refers to intense workout periods, typically ranging from days to months, during which the body is overloaded without adequate rest. The technique is akin to stretching a rubber band. The longer the band stretches, the bigger the rebound when it's let go.

During a training block, an athlete pushes to the point of utter exhaustion. Eventually, his performance drops off. But after a period of rest (in training lingo, tapering), during which the body overcompensates, the athlete experiences huge performance gains and, when timed right, is fresh for competition.

The danger lies in stretching the band too far, to the point where it snaps. For an athlete, not allowing enough rest will result in injury, sickness, or constant fatigue.

Instead of a typical training block of a few weeks or months, I view the next 3 years preceding Sydney as one giant training block. I do something to make myself better every day, even during my infrequent recovery periods. When I'm not lifting or doing intervals on my bike, I swim and do core work.

I vow not to rest until Sydney. I will punish myself day after day, year after year. When I finally release the rubber band and allow my body to realize the benefits of my hard work, I will ensure there are no photo finishes in Sydney.

I know this training plan will likely cost me dozens of World Cup wins, and probably a few world titles, but I don't care. I train right through World Cup races without resting. *Let my competitors rest and beat me now*, I think. They'll pay in Sydney.

At national-level competitions, I add work on top of the races. I train before and after my events. I even compete in endurance events, such as the points race, which a match sprinter would normally never enter. I grew up winning local road races, and I'm not afraid to take on the top US endurance riders. Frequently, I beat them.

I'm cognizant to the risks of this training plan. If I don't win gold in Sydney, I will surely regret the potential world championship wins I gave up by not tapering. Though I rely on Gil, and Andrzej, and even Erv for advice, I design my own training schedules. If my plan fails and I don't win gold, I alone will bear the responsibility.

. . . .

In '97, the world championships take place in Perth, Australia. Ever since my first individual senior worlds, in 1993, I've taken home a medal. Even in '95, when I raced with a broken kneecap, I won bronze in the team sprint. I arrive in Perth intent on continuing the streak. I won the final World Cup race of the season before coming to the world championships, but my training load has tired me during the course of the year.

The keirin tournament comes first. I breeze through the opening rounds and into the finals. In the keirin finals, Fiedler and Chiappa ride like maniacs. They hook and chop everyone in the race, and still don't win. Magné sneaks away with a lap to go for the victory. I finish a disappointing fifth. The race was so screwed up that most of the other riders, though not Magné, ask for a reride. But the officials instead decide to disqualify Fiedler and Chiappa from second and third. I'm awarded the bronze. My world championship medal streak continues, if only by consolation.

In the match sprint I fall to a Latvian whom I already dusted a number of times throughout the season. I don't even make the medal rounds. Publicly, I blame my gear selection for the loss. I rode a smaller 49-by-14 gear combination when a larger gear would've won me the race. But I always ride smaller gears in the early rounds of sprint tournaments. I save the bigger gears, and my legs, for the later rounds and faster competitors. I just didn't have the quickness to turn the smaller gear fast enough to win.

I never tell anyone why my performances occasionally suffer. I never use the workload under which I'm racing as an excuse. Instead, I view beating the best in the world, even when I'm tired, as a challenge. I only care about Sydney.

· · · · · · · · ·

I take a break from training just once a year, in the fall, during hunting season. The only time I can stop thinking about Atlanta is when I'm in the outdoors. I still hunt with Jay and my father, and our extended family of outdoorsmen. I also regularly hunt with Gil. We shoot turkeys, deer, pheasants, ducks, and geese. We hunt pretty much everything. We even kill the occasional black bear.

One benefit of my professional success and Olympic notoriety is the opportunity to hunt big game in some of the country's most idyllic locations and appear on celebrity hunting shows. Jim Kennedy invites me to Colorado to hunt mule deer. I'm asked to appear on an ESPN outdoors show with Larry Csonka. I also appear on television shows for the wetland conservation organization, Ducks Unlimited, and Rocky Mountain Elk Foundation.

Whether I'm hunting in Pennsylvania or some other remote location, the outdoors and the focused pursuit of a trophy animal remain an important part of my recovery process.

· · · · · · · · ·

Before the start of the '98 season, Erv and I go to a national team camp at the US Olympic Training Center in Colorado Springs. One day we're killing time between training sessions, shooting hoops in the gym when we witness something amazing.

An Olympic weight lifter named Mark Henry is playing on a hoop next to us. We can't help but notice him. He's a giant man with a thick beard and shoulder-length dreadlocks. He easily weighs 400 pounds.

All of a sudden Henry bursts straight off the ground and slams a basketball. The gym floor shakes as he lands.

I look at Erv. Our jaws drop. I can dunk a basketball, too, but neither of us can believe a man that big can get airborne. Then, another Olympic weight lifter, this one only 5 feet 5 inches tall does the same thing. He rockets toward the rim and dunks easily. He doesn't even take a running start.

I know the Olympic lifters are strong, but the explosiveness they display boggles my mind. It's the same type of strength I use during a sprint, power combined with quickness. I need to know what they're doing in the gym.

Erv and I track down their coach, a Romanian who won bronze at the '84 Olympics, Dragomir Cioroslan. At the height of his career, Cioroslan lifted twice his own 165-pound body weight. He talks to us about the various Olympic lifts and how to perform them properly. Technique is key, he says. Without proper form, we'll end up crushed beneath the bar. Explode into the lift, he says.

When I get back home, I invest in my own Olympic lifting setup. I contact John Brinson, the owner of a local gym called the West End Racquet Club. I tell him the lifts will be violent and loud and probably shock the other gym patrons, but they will help me win a gold medal. He agrees to give me my own workout room. I buy special rubber weights and install floor mats that I can drop the weight bar onto after each lift.

After the room is set up, Gil and I get to work. Gil's now my assistant, more than my coach. He helps rack the weights and prepare the bars for various lifts. He jokes that he's just my caddie. But I want him with me when I work out. He implicitly understands the toll a workout takes on my body and mind. No one is better at keeping me focused and psyching me up to put in an all-out effort than Gil.

I don't want any loose clothing snagging on the weight bar during the lifts, so I only wear a jock strap and a pair of spandex shorts, no shirt. Sweat pours off my chest and drips down on the bar as I prepare for a series of power cleans. I look down at the bar. On either end sits a stack of plates with a combined weight of 325 pounds. As I prepare for the vicious round of reps, I recall my childhood, and my mom's words: "No matter how hard you think you're working, someone is always working harder than you." I approach every lift like I sprint, like my life depends on it.

But the mind-set applies to more than just getting the weight off the ground. My livelihood as the world's best sprinter depends on each and every lift. With each rep, I'm building toward Sydney, gaining the power and quickness I will need to beat the best sprinters in the world. If I lose my focus, if I use poor technique or don't control the weight, I can seriously injure myself. Olympic lifters have dislocated their elbows in competition, crumpling to the ground with the bar falling on top of them. Gil doesn't spot me. If the weight slips, there's nothing he could do anyway. It's best he just stays out of the way. If I don't control the weight, I'm on my own.

I rub chalk between my hands, reach down, and grip the bar at a width slightly wider than my shoulders. My knees bend, my back rests at a 50-degree angle to my thighs, my abs contract, my glutes tighten. I look straight ahead.

Boom. I blast into the floor, extending my legs and back. The weight flies off the ground and moves directly upward. I catch the bar on my chest in a deep squat. One breath in, one breath out. *Boom.* Every muscle in my legs, butt, and back fires to move the bar upward again, pushing the massive weight against the force of gravity. I finish the lift standing, with my feet shoulder-width apart.

One rep down. I drop the bar to the floor. The rubber weights bounce three times, each one less high than the last. I reach down, move the bar back into position, and prepare for the second of a half dozen more reps.

With each completed power clean, pressure builds inside my

head. It feels as if I'm descending from 30,000 feet on an airplane. I can only vaguely hear Gil shouting, "C'mon Blade, dig in! Let's go! C'mon, push . . . get it! Don't quit, Blade! Go! Go! Go!" I finish my final rep and drop the bar. It rolls toward the wall. Gil hands me a bottle of water. I breathe deeply. My ears pop.

After a short break, I move on to the next set. At the end of the lifting session, after all the reps and sets of squats, deadlifts, and overhead presses after pools of sweat accumulate on the floor, and my hands are caked with the chalk, and Gil's hoarse from yelling, I've put up more than 50,000 pounds of weight.

· · · · · · · · ·

By the time I get home from the gym, I'm catatonic. I need rest. I need to sit nearly motionless and let my body recuperate as much as possible before that afternoon's sprint workout at the velodrome.

I'm home, but I'm not here. My physical presence is in the room, but I'm mentally detached. I seal myself off. Emotional connection requires too much effort.

Tyler is 3, and a bundle of energy. I look at him and smile. He's constantly up to something and into something—probably a lot like me at the same age. I love him, but I don't have the energy to give him the attention I should. I just lifted 25 tons. Now I can barely swing a 45-pound 3-year-old over my head. It pains me not to play with him. I want to chase him around the house for hours on end, listening to him giggle and scream. I want to feel that pure, parental joy. But I don't.

When athletes mention sacrifice, they don't talk about putting winning in front of their own family. But that's what I've done. I've missed most of Tyler's growing up because I was off racing or at some training camp. Now Christi is pregnant with our second child. She's due any day now, and she'll bear the early years of raising this child alone, as well. I tell myself in the end I'm doing this for my family. I promise myself I'll make it up to them when this is over—after I win gold. I use the long absences from my family as motivation.

I look into the foyer, where my silver medal from Atlanta sits. Christi proudly set it there right after we got home from the Olympics. Then we got in a fight.

"Put it away," I told her.

"No, it's something to be proud of," she said. "You worked hard for this."

"Not hard enough," I told her. But Christi didn't budge. It stayed in the foyer.

She leaves the case open, with the medal on display. I walk over to the medal and close the case. She'll open it back up tomorrow. She always does.

Christi asks me if I'm ready to eat. When I'm home she cooks all of my meals. She doesn't work. She treats taking care of Tyler and taking care of me as her job. My job is to train, eat, sleep—and then win. Her commitment to winning gold in Sydney matches my own. I never touch a spatula or turn on a stovetop. She sometimes even pours the milk over my cereal in the morning.

I can't perform at the top level of the sport alone. Christi is part of my team, the people around me who help me succeed—my family and my training staff. Gil and Andrzej help me train and are my corner men during competitions. Eddie works the thick knots out of my muscles with those big hands. Christi makes our home a completely stress-free environment—a place where I'm allowed to be lazy. Tyler is one of the few people who can make me smile.

Christi finds fulfillment in working toward our mutual goal, but like me, she also experiences isolation. She's lonely. People don't understand her commitment to my success. Social interactions often end awkwardly. Friends say she's spoiling me. They don't see how taking care of my every need makes me perform better. They've never won an Olympic medal. They've never lost gold.

I'm not always there for her, either. When I'm home, I don't talk to her about my training or my races. I live two lives, one with her and Tyler and another fighting my demons in the gym and on the track. I know it's not fair to her, but I can't bring my demons home with me. My home is my sanctuary. Even though I'm her husband, Christi finds out how my races went from people who read about me in the paper.

When I'm in the middle of a brutal stretch of training, our daily interactions sometimes devolve to just hello and goodbye. Or, when's the next meal?

One day, overwhelmed with frustration, Christi says to me, "You know, it's been months since we've had a real conversation."

I don't know what to say. I just say, "I don't want to lose you over this."

But Christi keeps things from me, too. Any issues that arise around the house she deals with alone. She doesn't tell me if Tyler's sick. If he kept her up all night, crying. She doesn't want to distract me. Even joyful moments, like Tyler's first words, she keeps from me until I return home.

I talk with her on the phone, and I hear the kids crying. I ask her what's wrong, why are they crying? She doesn't tell me they're crying because I'm not home. She knows I feel bad about missing the seminal events in my kids' lives, and that if I truly knew how much it meant to them, it might affect my focus and determination.

She understands that I have to put myself first. So she puts me before herself.

I don't know if I could make the same sacrifice for someone else.

11

DISAPPOINTMENT IN BORDEAUX

DURING THE winter of '98, I'm finishing off a training ride by riding up the gradual hill toward my house. The computer on my handlebars reads 49.73 miles. I'm not happy with this number. My goal is to win gold in Sydney. I am number one, I tell myself. I will not end a ride with any number other than the number one.

I turn into our long driveway, 50.28 miles. I reach the garage door, 50.43. I roll back down the driveway and turn around until I'm at 50.88. Christi comes out of the house and sees me doing circles in front of the garage door. "What are you doing?" she asks. My bike's odometer ticks over to 51. I'm satisfied.

"Finishing my ride," I say, as I roll my bike into the garage. I don't tell Christi how obsessive I've become. Christi does enough. She doesn't need to bear this burden with me. I'm possessed by my drive to win in Sydney. I'm in a trance.

The compulsion overtakes my every action. I pump 11.11 gallons of gas. I take one drink from the water fountain. The mind-set becomes an obsession. I make sure my seats on airplanes and my hotel rooms contain the number one. I end every ride on the number one. I am number one.

· · · · · · · · ·

Later in the winter I go to Dallas for a training camp with my trade team, EDS. In Dallas, Erv and I lift weights at the Tom Landry Fitness Center at Baylor Hospital. In addition to its immaculate weight facilities, the Fitness Center does performance testing, everything from maximum VO_2 analysis to hydrostatic body fat testing, also known as the dip tank. I decide to measure my body fat in the dip tank.

The dip tank uses a scale placed inside a tub of water to measure a person's buoyancy. Because body fat floats, and muscle and bone sink, the difference between a person's weight in the water and his or her weight on dry land provides the most accurate measurement of body fat percentage. I strip down to my shorts, get onto the scale in the tub, and submerge myself underwater, blowing out all the excess air in my lungs. The scale measures my weight under water. An algorithm that compares my water weight to my standard weight calculates my body fat.

Even though it's early in the season and I'm not even close to my peak fitness, I don't like the results. I'm 8 percent body fat, a number well within the range of most world-class sprinters. But I aim to win the Olympics, and 8 percent means I can improve. If I'm carrying less fat on my muscle-bound body, I can accelerate more quickly. I need to get quicker. Fiedler beat me not because he was faster or stronger, but because I couldn't get past him in the final 100 meters. He beat me off the line and protected the front with his superior quickness. I'm one of the three quickest sprinters in the world. I need to be number one.

When I get back home to the Lehigh Valley, I tell Christi to clean out the kitchen. Get rid of the junk, I say. I grew up in a PA Dutch family, where baked treats and fatty meats were the norm. A traditional PA Dutch salad consists of iceberg lettuce drowned in hot bacon dressing. Growing up, my family considered all food healthy. Though we ate venison regularly, we never thought of it as a healthy, lean meat. We ate venison because we hunted deer. My parents never discussed empty calories, or good versus bad fat. If the food filled you up and kept you working hard, it was good food.

In college, Tim Quigley and I regularly got our dinner from the local convenience store. We considered a few packs of Twinkies and a giant soda a well-rounded meal. At the Alpine training camp, Erv and I drank super-caffeinated Jolt sodas and ate king-size candy bars during our rides. Many of those bad dietary habits stuck with me. I eat ice cream almost every night. I crave Wendy's hamburgers when I'm traveling. *I work hard enough to eat whatever I want*, I think.

But not if I want to win the Olympics. We throw out the candy bars I sometimes eat and the potato chips and the soft drinks. Christi reads through an array of nutrition books. She cooks homemade meals with the right amounts of carbohydrates, protein, and fat. Food is fuel, she says. The quality of the fuel, and when you fill up, makes all the difference when it comes to performing better and getting leaner.

Christi prepares the right meals at exactly the right times. More carbs in advance of my workouts to provide quick-burning energy, and balanced dishes with lean protein to aid recovery afterward. She makes peanut butter, banana, and honey sandwiches on whole wheat bread as my favorite prerace snacks and cooks dinners with the lean meats I stockpile each hunting season. We never eat after 7 p.m. I don't touch alcohol.

As the diet takes hold, fat fades away from parts of my body where I didn't even know it existed. My muscly quads go from looking just big to freakishly defined. Veins pop out of my shoulders and make a web across my abs.

I was 225 pounds in Atlanta. I go down to 210, and I gain power in the gym and on the track. The next time I get in a dip tank, I'm just 4.5 percent body fat. I almost feel sorry for the racers who will face me in Sydney.

Almost.

· · · · · · · · ·

In the summer I head back to Texas for the national championships in Frisco, a suburb north of Dallas. The sponsor of my team, EDS, recently spent $4 million to construct a state-of-the-art track in Frisco, dubbed the Superdrome.

The Superdrome is a modern marvel, designed and built by the same company that made the Atlanta velodrome. It's 250 meters around with ridiculously steep 44-degree turns and composite boards that *whoosh* under my bike wheels. Personally, I don't like the track. It's too similar to the Olympic velodrome. When I ride the track, I'm reminded of losing gold.

Nick Chenowth, the director of the EDS cycling team, helped convince the company to build the Superdrome in partnership with local governments. The track represents the crown jewel of a cycling empire Nick built and now oversees. Since the '96 Games, the EDS team has grown from a group of employees who liked to race bikes into perhaps the most talent-laden track cycling team in the world.

After the Atlanta Games, Erv decided to switch over to road cycling, but Nick convinced him to come back to the track and race for EDS. Nick gave Erv a contract so good, Erv even decided to buy a house in the Dallas area, near the track. Nick also signed former Olympic medalist and former world champion Rebecca Twigg.

The EDS team rides the nicest equipment available. Inside the team's sparkling trailer sits an array of carbon-fiber track bikes and wheels, top-of-the-line handmade gear. EDS also sponsors a national series of track races around the country and handles the computer systems at USA Cycling in a sponsorship deal worth more than half a million dollars.

Some people might contend that the amount of money EDS pumps into track cycling doesn't necessarily make sense. Why would a technology company care so much about supporting track racing? But no one says anything. Nick, who's also the head of the company's international sports marketing division, convinces anyone who'll listen that EDS is getting a deal. The company will easily earn back its investment when EDS racers make it to the Olympics. We all buy what Nick sells. Heck, we're getting paid to.

· · · · · · · · ·

I train straight through nationals, and still win three more US titles. Then I head to Blaine, Minnesota, for another training camp in advance of the '98 world championships in Bordeaux, France. I'm ripping apart the track in Minnesota, riding unofficial world-record times, even during the last few intervals of my brutal workouts.

I want to make the times count. I convince Gil and Andrzej to give me a crack at a world record. We call in an official from the international governing body for sports cycling, the UCI (International Cycling Union), to clock me. We get US Olympic Committee drug testers at the track. I aim to break the world record for 500 meters.

But Andrzej won't let me miss a second of training to set this record. We schedule the record attempt for Wednesday night, at the end of my evening training session, and after a morning workout that same day.

Wednesday evening comes. It's August in Minnesota, but unseasonably cool as the sun dips below the track's railing. A blustery wind blows across my bare shins as I circle the top of the boards, preparing to launch my record-setting ride. I'll ride two laps as fast as I can around the track. I ignore the soreness in my quads from the day's hard work and focus on the final, intense effort I will make for just under a half minute.

I approach the start line and drop from the top of the track all the way to the black line ringing the inside of the boards. I stand and pound on the pedals until I reach my max speed. The first lap flies past, effortlessly. I'm topping out at 45 miles per hour as I cross the start–finish line to start the second lap.

Some people might interpret the surge of lactic acid flowing through my body as pain. But I don't hurt. I'm floating. I'm in complete control of my body and my bike.

I whip through the final turn as if I'm riding a set of rails, my bike pinned against the bottom edge of the track. My legs spin as fast as humanly possible. I cross the line. 26.482 seconds. A full 0.2 seconds faster than the previous mark, set by a Russian sprinter more than 10 years ago—but still not as fast as times I set during training.

. . . .

I head to worlds brimming with confidence, but still not willing to back off my demanding training schedule. Worlds take place in Bordeaux, amid a strangely intense atmosphere. Everyone seems on edge, as if a full moon is lighting the velodrome.

My world record, and the publicity it spawned, caught the attention of the racing world. Record attempts are typically made in the thin air of high-altitude velodromes. Rarely does a record fall on an outdoor, sea level track like Blaine's. The other racers know I'm hauling ass. I'm the favorite.

In the quarterfinals of the match sprint, I meet Darryn Hill. The Australian national team, including Hill, spent the summer in T-Town and we raced regularly on Friday nights. We waged some intense battles on the T-Town track. But those were friendly bouts compared to the intensity we bring to the world championships.

In Bordeaux, we revert to our most hardened demeanors. I want to kill him. He wants to kill me. I ready myself for a cage match. All eyes turn to the track when we line up. Racers stop warming up on their rollers. The officials become more vigilant. They know it won't be a clean race.

Hill wins the first ride. I must win the next two rides to make it to the semifinal round. In the second ride, he moves high in the final turn and leaves the sprinter's lane open. I drop underneath him. Hill retaliates by dropping down the banking, right into me. We're shoulder to shoulder coming into the finishing straight.

Hill keeps moving to his left, forcing me onto the apron. As we approach the line, both of us are riding completely off the wooden boards, now waging our battle out-of-bounds. I lean to my right and headbutt Hill in the shoulder to push him back up onto the track as we cross the finish line.

The officials relegate Hill. I get the win.

We line up for the third ride. The winner makes the medal round. Hill leads off the line. Coming into the last lap we wind up our sprints. I fake as if I'm going to sprint over the top of Hill. He throws me a hook coming into the first turn, trying to beat me back, but I'm not there. I've dropped underneath him. When he realizes I'm coming below him, Hill tries to chop down on me. But he's too late.

I'm already in front of Hill, and retaliating with my own hook, whipping my rear wheel up the banking as we exit the second turn. He tries to dodge me, but he's late again. *Zzzzing!* I shave off a piece of his shoe with the bladed spokes on my wheel and slice one of his leather toe straps in half.

I win uncontested. Hill runs his mouth after we cross the line.

"You nearly took my fucking toes off!" Hill shouts in his thick Aussie accent.

Back in the cabins, the giant German sprinter Michael Hübner takes up Hill's argument. He's shouting at the officials to disqualify me. Never mind that he's got no affiliation with Australia, and isn't even racing. He obviously doesn't realize how much I love to scrap. I dismount my bike and head for our team's cabin. "Fuck off," I yell over at Hübner from the US team's cabin.

Hübner refocuses his rage on me. He moves toward me, I move toward him—two 200-plus-pound men preparing to collide. The laws of physics attest this will not end well. I charge right through the waist-high metal barricades trying to reach Hübner. But before we can meet, Gil jumps in front of me. The German contingent grabs Hübner. We're steered in opposite directions.

The next day I lose to Florian Rousseau in the semifinal of the match sprints.

After the race, I'm called in for the compulsory drug testing. I'm seething. I expected to win, and I didn't. In the testing room, I can't pee. A half hour passes, then 90 minutes, as I wait to go. A frustrated French drug-testing official sighs and looks at his watch. "Oh geez," he says. I snap. I throw the piss cup across the room. A stack of documents sitting on a desk goes flying. I can't believe I didn't win. I'm the world record holder.

In the keirin, the last event at worlds, I place fourth in my semifinal heat. Only the top three advance to the finals. I don't have any power left in my legs. Three weeks ago, in Blaine, I was the best in the world, ever. I guaranteed a win in Bordeaux, and I arrived prepared to do just that. But I didn't. My streak of 5 consecutive years with at least one world championship medal ends in Bordeaux.

· · · · · · · · ·

That evening, Erv and I decide to go over to the race hotel and hang out. As soon as we get there, I run into Hill. He stares me down. I stare back. Moments later we're face to face, nose to nose, daring each other to toss a jab. I can smell the cheap French beer on his breath.

"You messed up," Hill says, claiming I fouled him in the last ride.

"No, you messed up," I counter. It was he who tried to chop me first.

"Let's go outside and settle this," Hill says.

"Let's go," I say.

Hill stands at least 4 inches shorter than me, but he's nearly as wide as he is tall—built like a concrete pillar. He's also a thug who's been convicted for assault in the past. But I won't back down from anyone, especially another sprinter, especially right now.

Erv and a semicircle of spectators stare at us in disbelief. If these two guys fight, someone will surely die, they think. Just before Hill and I turn to walk outside, Erv and few other racers finally jump in between us. "Whoa, c'mon guys," Erv says. He knows I'll regret the altercation. No one wins in a fight like this. Hill and I move in separate directions.

But the fight continues inside me.

I'm an Olympian, a hero to thousands, a father to two adorable children, and a husband to a beautiful wife. My closest friends—my team—are the ones who make my success possible. But it's letting down this very team that makes me madder than ever after Bordeaux. They sacrificed for me, and I didn't come through.

Just like in Atlanta.

12
—
DO THE RIGHT THING

IN THE WINTER of 1999, I attend a training camp in Dallas with the EDS team. Despite the unseasonably warm weather and our daily sessions on the beautiful new Superdrome track, an air of ambiguity hangs over the group. EDS recently replaced its bike racing–friendly CEO with a new executive, a known cost-cutter. Rumors swirl among the riders that EDS will pull the sponsorship plug. I try to brush them off and focus on business as usual—training.

But I'm not immune to the speculation. I'm in the midst of contract negotiations with the team manager, Nick Chenowth. He's certain I'll win gold in Sydney, only about 18 months away now. He wants to sign me through 2004, before my price skyrockets. I'm eager to ink a new deal, too.

Nick's extravagance—some would say arrogance—rubs a lot of people the wrong way, including my teammate, Chris Carlson, a member of the employee team and a lawyer at EDS. Nick personifies a stereotype common to Dallas. He wears designer suits and drives ridiculous cars. He recently traded his Lamborghini in for a Ferrari. His über-modern home is decked out with expensive Cantoni furniture.

But my own experiences with Nick (excepting our tandem crashes) remain positive. He's a consummate salesman, which is something I can relate to, having grown up around the auto retail industry. Watching him pitch his sports-marketing projects to a room full of EDS executives wearing intimidating dark suits is awe-inspiring.

Nick's enthusiasm for the EDS cycling team is infectious, even among the riders. The team is a mix of full-time athletes like Erv and me, plus company employees like Carlson. Despite our seemingly different agendas, members of the team rally around one another at events. When Carlson sets the national pursuit record at a big track race, I slap him on the back. "Bad ass, Chris," I say. "Way to ride your bike!"

More than anything, though, Nick believes in me. He insists he wants to wrap me up before the Sydney Games, but he hesitates on drawing up a new contract. For the first time in our relationship, he lacks confidence at the negotiating table.

During the camp, I also have a strange conversation with Steve Walsh, who works with Nick in the Global Sports division at EDS. I consider Steve a friend and our conversation is jovial.

"Hey, did you get a check for $10,000 from Nick?" he asks. "He said he needed the money for a business deal you two were working on together."

"No," I say, befuddled. *Maybe I didn't account for a bonus?* I think. I'll keep a close eye on the mail from now on, I jokingly tell Steve.

Something's up, but I don't know exactly what.

Later, I go on a road ride with Gil, whom Nick hired as an EDS coach this year. Gil's excited about his new position. He's always measured the rewards of coaching through the success of his athletes. But finally, Gil is receiving compensation proportionate to his talent as a trainer and motivator.

Me, I'm not so chipper. I turn and look over at Gil while we ride. He sees the pessimism on my face. "This could all be gone in the blink of an eye," I say.

· · · · · · · · ·

In March, just before the racing season starts, the ax falls. The new CEO cuts EDS's Global Sports division, meaning the company will no longer sponsor the cycling team that pays my salary. Suddenly, I'm unemployed. But I'm not the only one affected.

EDS sponsors every facet of track cycling in the United States. Gil loses his job, and so does Erv. The sport's governing body, USA Cycling, relied on EDS for nearly $1 million worth of sponsorship every year. That's gone. The EDS Cup, a nationwide series of track races, comes to an abrupt end. Without a title sponsor, even the recently constructed Superdrome near Dallas, which EDS invested in heavily, faces an uncertain future.

I can't say I'm surprised. Maybe I somehow jinxed the team with my comments to Gil a few weeks earlier. I don't know what will happen to my current contract, which pays me through 2000, and if I'll be able afford the mortgage on my new home. But I'm determined not to let the EDS fallout distract me from my goal: winning the Olympics.

I call Gil moments after we get the disheartening news.

"I'm going to the gym," I say. "You coming?"

"Not today," he says. He's just not in the mood.

I take out my frustration on the weights. I thrash my body with set after vicious set of Olympic-style lifts. I throw up more weight, and with greater intensity, than I have all year.

In some ways I feel liberated. I'm free of the financial motivation to compete. As I toss the immense weight around the gym, the pressure builds inside my head. I remember my childhood and brashly proclaiming, "I'm going to win the Olympics someday!" Sweat pours down my shoulders and cakes on the chalk in my palms. I think back to the day Jay and I tossed those rocks—*Thwack! Thwack! Thwack!*—the day I first discovered bike racing in the basement of Heinz's house.

I'm destined to race track bikes in the Olympic Games. It doesn't matter if I earn millions of dollars or a single cent. My silver medal still haunts me. I still dream of winning gold. As I finish the last rep in a set of power cleans, I let out a scream—a war cry—that echoes off of the thick concrete walls. I release the weights, flicking them away from my body and letting them fall to the rubber mats where they bounce a few times.

I stand stoically for a moment, alone in the brick room. The sweat rolls off the tips of my fingers and into small pools on the black floor. My legs and ass, my lower back and abs, my chest and shoulders, even my neck, throb with fatigue. My body aches that good ache of a job well done—a workout that will reap dividends.

I can't wait to get to Sydney.

A few days later Gil shows up at the gym.

"I'm with you," he says. "Let's get after it."

·　·　·　·　·　·　·　·　·

Since Atlanta, I often struggle getting to sleep. I lie in bed, thinking about what I can do to get quicker. Sometimes, visions wake me in the middle of the night. I see Fiedler in front of me. I charge at his rear wheel. He holds me off. I can't get around him. I am one of the quickest sprinters in the world. I need to be the quickest. I stare into the darkness of the night, trying to figure out how.

Then one day, I'm flipping though my local newspaper, the *Morning Call*, when I spot an ad for athletic speed camps. I pick up the phone and call the number. A man named Ed Ruisz answers. He tells me he is a native Pennsylvanian and ran track in college during the '80s. In school, his graduate work in human performance took him to the Soviet Union, where he studied at the Soviet Sports Institute in Moscow. Upon returning to the Lehigh Valley, Ruisz brought back the Eastern Bloc training techniques the Soviets and East Germans used to dominate track cycling, before the Berlin Wall fell in 1989. He tells me he can make me quicker.

Though his methods seem unorthodox, Ruisz's athletes get results. As the track coach at a local high school, Ruisz's women's team set a national record for consecutive victories. His team won 134 track meets in a row. In his spare time Ruisz works with NFL players and other professional athletes.

Now, he'll train me.

Ruisz says to get quicker, I must train my mind as well as my body. We start with plyometric exercises. Basically, jumping. But Ruisz doesn't just tell me to start a round of plyometrics. Every movement I perform is keyed by a visual stimulus. Ruisz signals me to begin the exercise by flashing a light, teaching my body to react without waiting for a conscious order from my brain.

Ruisz attaches surgical tubing to a belt on my waist. He makes me perform vertical leaps and standing long jumps against the stretchy resistance, slowing my reaction time to the start signal. Then, Ruisz takes away the resistance, letting me respond instantaneously. Next, he straps me into ankle shackles and instructs me to do a series of split-jump squats. I start in a forward lunge position, then leap into the air and alternate legs. During the jump squats, the shear force expended by my powerful legs frequently causes the elastic bands to snap in half. We remedy this problem by using two sets of elastic bands for many of the exercises I perform.

To recruit more of the fast-twitch muscle fibers required of my explosive sprint efforts, Ruisz uses the elastic bands to tow me as I run. The short bursts of running, performed with the aid of the elastic instead of against it, force me to turn my legs over faster. Where I would normally run 20 meters in just under 3 seconds without the elastic towing me, it takes me just 2.5 seconds with the elastic.

Ruisz's training flies in the face of traditional practices for cycling, namely the notion that bike racers don't run. But I'm confident that Ruisz knows how to make athletes quicker. I work out beside football stars, whose sport requires lightning-fast reactions, and I regularly outperform them.

As the season progresses, Gil and I adapt Ruisz's quickness techniques to the bike. Gil flashes a light to signal the start of a sprint interval, or he simply waves his hand in my peripheral vision. The drills mimic the type of quickness I need to keep a competitor from jumping over the top of me in a race, or beating me off the line.

The lapse between the message from my brain and response from my body nearly disappears. Everything seems to slow down. I can grab fish from flowing streams and snatch flies out of the air.

· · · · · · · · ·

After EDS pulls out, my friend Jim Kennedy, of Cox Enterprises, steps in to help. He pays me to race for a team sponsored by one of his subsidiary businesses, AutoTrader.com, which is managed by another friend of mine, Macon Cherp. I earn enough to focus on the Olympics, without worrying about refinancing my house.

But the drama with EDS isn't over. I get another phone call from Steve asking about unaccounted-for money, involving Nick. I conclude EDS is looking into the cycling team's finances. And the bizarre nature of Steve's questions leads me to think they won't like what they find.

Not too long after Steve's call, I learn the company is investigating Nick for embezzlement. One of the lawyers working on the inquiry is my former teammate, Chris Carlson, who's accustomed to rooting out malfeasance within the company.

I later find out that Carlson is tenacious in his pursuit of Nick. In an effort to compile evidence, Carlson pores over the team's financial documents. He interviews, and in some cases deposes, nearly everyone involved with the EDS cycling team, from the prior CEO of the company to the manager of the local bike shop. Carlson even contacts the FBI, which considers pursuing criminal charges against Nick.

It doesn't take Carlson long to discover how Nick lived so lavishly. He submitted falsified expense reports to EDS for various goods and services. Most of the invoices and receipts for the goods were handwritten by Nick himself. The company then wrote Nick checks that were deposited directly into his personal account. Between 1994 and 1998, he stole well over $1 million from EDS.

Some of the expenses EDS erroneously paid for on behalf of the cycling team were for items that don't even exist, such as a set of 130-centimeter crankarms (most crankarms are measured in millimeters) and $12,000 for some mysterious bike containers. Nick supposedly purchased thousands of racing tires priced at more than $300 apiece, and bought bikes for the team that no one ever actually saw.

During the course of his investigation, Carlson alleges Nick used EDS money to buy those exotic sports cars and Italian furniture. He also alleges Nick stole $25,000 to pay for his girlfriend's boob job. But Carlson admits much of the money Nick took simply disappeared.

Then, one day, the EDS legal department contacts me. They want to talk to me; can I please come to Dallas? I've got nothing to hide. My lawyer, Eric Hall, who also acts as my agent, tells me not to worry. "There's not a scintilla of evidence you did anything wrong," he says. "Just be truthful." When I sit down with the EDS lawyers, I make sure Carlson's there. He knows cycling, and he attests that I was in no way involved in Nick's fraud.

Eventually, the case goes to civil court. Nick acknowledges his guilt to the judge and agrees to pay $1.3 million in restitution to EDS. Then, the FBI files its criminal case. The saga finally ends when Nick is sentenced to 27 months in a federal prison.

Though I absolutely don't condone Nick's actions, I'm less hard on him than many people. During its height, EDS was the best track-cycling team in the world, and the company's support of USA Cycling gave opportunities to athletes they would've otherwise never imagined.

Nick also believed steadfastly in me. You are going to win the Olympics one day, he would tell me. Though many people consider Nick to be a scoundrel, he helped me to believe in myself. Unfortunately, it was that same talent to make people believe, as well as Nick's own greed, that caused his downfall.

Publicly, Nick continues to dispute any wrongdoing.

. . . .

In August of 1999, I put the EDS fiasco behind me and head to Winnipeg, Canada, for the Pan-Am Games. The competition will serve as the selection for the Sydney Olympics. Just before the Pan-Am Games, I set max lifts in the gym as I continue to get more lean. I put up 550 pounds on the squat rack and lift 315 pounds 10 times on the bench press.

I'm ready to kick some ass. This is the moment I've waited for since Atlanta. The run into Sydney has begun. For the first time in nearly 3 years, I rest. I back off of my training and let my body recover from the repeated beatings I've given it in the gym and on the track, year after year.

When cyclists taper for a big race, they talk about letting themselves breathe. As if the training prior to the event was suffocation, and taking a rest feels like breathing big gulps of air. For years, I drowned myself with training. Now, I'm rising to the surface. After the disappointment of worlds in Bordeaux and the EDS debacle, I'm angry. Really angry. I'm ready to annihilate my competitors.

Heading into the Pan-Am Games, I'm also excited. Win these races, and I'm guaranteed a trip to Sydney. In the match sprints I qualify first, and set a Pan-Am record for the flying 200 meters at 10.3 seconds. I dominate each of my opponents in the early rounds of the sprint tournament, and meet another American, Marcelo Arrue, in the final. Arrue is a good friend and teammate of mine. He even moved to T-Town and is a valued training partner. But he's no match for me in competition. I beat Arrue in two straight rides.

Though I'm not competing in the team sprint in Sydney, I offer to race the event at the Pan-Am Games and help the team earn another spot for the Games. I combine with Arrue and Johnny Bairos. We win handedly, beating Cuba by more than a second.

In the keirin, I take off from the front as soon as the pace bike pulls off the track. I sprint for two and a half laps, simply riding away from everyone else in the race. I'm the first athlete to ever win three gold medals at the Pan-Am Games.

My ticket to Sydney is punched.

· · · · · · · · ·

I've accomplished my goal for the year, qualifying for the Olympics. I'm ready to end my season and start my final preparations for Sydney, the only race I care about. I plan on skipping worlds in September, but USA Cycling pressures me to compete. If I race, I can help the US team earn more spots for the Olympics, the Feds tell me.

I consider myself extremely loyal, and attending worlds will give me a chance to repay my teammates, my friends, who are instrumental as training partners. I agree to race, and travel to Berlin for worlds.

When the match-sprint tournament starts, I'm mentally unprepared. I'm fit physically, but in my head I'm ready for an off-season hunting trip. I struggle in the early rounds, then run into Fiedler in the quarterfinals. He dances around me on the track and convincingly beats me in two straight rides. Coming off the high of my Pan-Am performance, I don't want to end my season this way.

I refocus for the keirin, and dominate the qualifying rounds. During the semifinal race, I start my sprint from the back of the group and blow by everyone on the last lap. I'm confident I can win in the finals. I just have to beat Fiedler.

Worlds are in Berlin, Fiedler's home soil. He's desperate for a world title after narrowly losing the gold-medal round of the match sprint. As we prepare to line up for the keirin finals, Gil comes over and whispers into my ear. "Fiedler wants to make a deal," he says. I'll get $8,000 if I lead Fiedler out in the sprint and help him win a gold medal on his home turf.

Though it may seem unsportsmanlike to outsiders, paying off competitors isn't an uncommon practice in bike racing. Tour de France stages are often bought and sold on the run into the finish. With so many variables involved in a keirin, the top racers frequently try to limit the odds against them by forming combines. With his vast racing experience, Gil's accustomed to working out these kinds of deals.

The prospect of cutting a deal tempts me. Eight thousand dollars is a good amount of money. I could still get second or third and triple that amount with the incentives from my sponsors for being on the podium at a world championship. But I still want to win this race. It's not worth it.

Gil goes to back Fiedler's people, then back to me. Now they're offering $12,000, he tells me. I consider it. But I tell Gil, I still want to win. He tells Fiedler's people and comes back to me again. By this point, I'm taking my position on the start line, plotting out my strategy. "Fifteen thousand to lead out," Gil says.

I lean over my handlebars and close my eyes. I grip the drops of my bars and squeeze tight. The fallout from EDS taught me the only certainty in professional cycling is uncertainty. Under my new contract, I'm making a quarter of what I'm accustomed to. Take your money while you can get it, part of me thinks. But opting for the quick, easy, and unethical payoff never leads to long-term success. Nick showed me that.

My dad taught me that. "Do the right thing," he told me, over and over. "It will always catch up with you if you don't. Always."

If I win, I'll earn more from my sponsor incentives than Fiedler is offering. Plus, you cannot put a price tag on a world championship. It's a gamble, but it won't cost me my soul. I decide to bet on myself. "I'm going to go win this bike race," I say to Gil. "Fuck them. No deal."

The race starts. I'm third wheel as the pace bike trots around the track. Fiedler's tucked in behind me, shadowing me. The pace bike pulls off. Two and a half laps to go. I move into the lead. Behind me, I sense chaos. I can hear the other racers flying up and down the banking, jostling for position. The boards ache and moan underneath their wheels. I don't want to lead this race, but I don't want to fight either. I stay out of the turbulence.

Then, to my sudden relief, Magné comes from last wheel, all the way over the top. He pulls in front of me with a lap and a half to go. I couldn't buy a better position.

We come through for the bell lap at more than 40 miles per hour. I peek behind me. Fiedler rides inches off my rear wheel. But he must come around me, and Magné, to win. We exit the second corner and hit the back straight. Fiedler, Magné, and I pounce out of our saddles simultaneously. Magné's at the bottom of the track, I'm at his shoulder, Fiedler's at my hip. We are three wide across the steep banking as we whip off the back straight and fly through turns three and four.

As we exit the final turn, Magné tires. I pull into the lead, flying toward the line. Fiedler's coming fast. He's at my shoulder, he's beside me. There's the line. We throw our bikes. Arms forward, heads down, mirror images of each other.

· · · · · · · · ·

It's a dark, quiet plane ride back to the United States. I'm fuming. I raced the keirin clean, but Fiedler had home-field advantage—a joker in the deck. Before they even looked at the photo finish to definitively see who won, the German officiating staff disqualified me. It was bullshit. Even Fiedler said so. Andrzej appealed the official's decision, but they didn't reverse the call. Worst of all, my DQ was unnecessary. The finish-line shot clearly showed Fiedler nipping me on the line. He won by the width of a front tire.

After the race, my terrible temper got the best of me. I took out my frustration on the US team's cabin, leaving a melee of broken furniture and bike parts in my wake.

We raced like champions—no deals—and he beat me outright. I can live with that. I can't bear coming home empty-handed. No medal. No cash. Just my pride.

"I should've taken the deal and led Fiedler out," I tell Gil. But I don't really believe what I'm saying.

One year to Sydney, I think. One year until I'm number one.

Part 3

13
—
THE BLADE IS COMING

IN 1898 my great-grandfather competed in a road race in Egypt, Pennsylvania, near Allentown, near where I live now. At the time of his race, competitive cycling was booming in popularity across the United States.

Despite the unwieldy nature of the rudimentary bikes ridden at the time, hundreds of cycling competitions took place up and down the East Coast and across the Midwest. The events were held on roads composed of loose cobblestones and strewn with dirt, as well as on cinder tracks built for horse-and-buggy racing.

At the turn of the century, no sport drew spectators more rabid than bike-racing fans. In Egypt, hundreds of people flocked to the center of town an hour and a half before the start of the race, clamoring to see my great-grandfather take on the best cyclists in the area. When, after 52 minutes aboard his high-wheel bike, he broke the finishing tape, taking first place, the crowd roared and hoisted him up on their shoulders.

But my great-grandfather wasn't just a champion bike racer. He was also a fighter and a showman. He traveled extensively, often securing his room and board by holding impromptu, bare-knuckle boxing matches. Directly after his victory in Egypt, he boxed against a friend of his to prove how little energy the race had cost him.

The citizens of Egypt celebrated my great-grandfather's victory well into the evening. They placed a tall silk hat atop his head and paraded him through the streets in a carriage. My great-grandfather was given a brand-new bicycle as a prize.

I share my great-grandfather's name, Martin Nothstein. I also, undoubtedly, share his athleticism and tenacity. Like him, I'm compelled not just to compete and win, but to assert my superiority. I don't crave the adulation of others. I don't care if I'm loved or despised. But I need to be the best, and I need everyone to know it.

Unlike during the era of my great-grandfather, more than a century later, on the cusp of the 2000 Sydney Olympics, most Americans still know little about bike racing and even less about track cycling. The mainstream media pays attention to bike racing once a year, during the Tour de France. But track cycling lacks a Tour de France–type event to draw the eyes of the world every year. Prior to the Games, the sport's most mainstream publication, *Bicycling* magazine, did a feature story about me titled, "Marty the Obscure." The headline's point: In track cycling, only the Olympics matter.

The Olympics are track cycling's Tour de France. The Games are the only time the best in the world come together, and everyone in the world watches. In Sydney, I will make sure the entire world knows—I'm number one.

. . . .

I fly into Australia a full month before the Games. I will train and acclimate to the Southern Hemisphere at a camp held by the national team on the Gold Coast, in Brisbane, about 500 miles north of Sydney.

Unlike in '96, the US cycling team is not highly touted coming into the Sydney Olympics. After the collapse of EDS, USA Cycling's focus, and most of their monetary investment, turned to the road. I'm the sole medal hope for the entire track team—and given my mixed results over the previous 4 years, I'm no longer considered the favorite. *Sports Illustrated* picks me for the bronze medal in 2000.

A year has gone by since my close loss, and disqualification, to Fiedler in the keirin at worlds. Though the previous 3 years passed in a blur of determined training, racing, and travel, the year preceding Sydney has been one of constant anticipation. I've purposely tried to stay off my competitors' radar, racing very little, and mostly training alone with just Gil and Eddie at my side.

I started the 2000 season with a winter boot camp in Charleston, South Carolina. No family, no teammates, no national team coaches, no distractions. Just Gil, Eddie, and me—training every day for a month. A friend of Eddie's, named Artur Pacult, who lives in Charleston, graciously hosted us. Artur is a neurosurgeon and a cycling aficionado. We share a deep appreciation of the sport's history. He got us access to Charleston Southern University, where I lifted weights and could perform key, preseason physiological testing. The camp was the perfect way to start my run toward Sydney.

But now, in this final month before the Games, time creeps along. I'm focused so sharply on the Olympics that everything in my field of vision appears blurred, except for the gold medal.

My single-mindedness makes me intolerable to everyone around me. Gil lives in constant fear of messing something up and ruining my shot at Olympic glory. Christi is as much a member of my training staff as she is my wife. My son, Tyler, and my 2-year-old daughter, Devon, barely know me. After I snap at my mom during a family gathering, she resolves not to speak to me unless spoken to.

I'm not a good person—people outside my small circle don't enjoy my company, and I don't enjoy theirs, either—but I'm riding faster than at any time in my life. I competed in just one World Cup race the entire year—Cali, Colombia. I dominated the match sprint, then didn't attend another international event all year. I let my competition stew on my forceful victory, while I tapered for Sydney.

As I drew down my training load and intensity, my body responded with a never-before-seen level of fitness. I'm more powerful, and quicker, than at any point in my life. Defeating my opponents is not enough. I aim to dominate them.

During the previous 3 years, my training left me in a fatigue-induced fog—never fully aware of my true capacity. But as Sydney approaches, and I reap the rewards of resting, I emerge from my haze.

Excess energy and adrenaline flow through me, making me twitchy and even more irritable. I'm a coiled snake, ready to strike.

A week before leaving for Australia, I tested my form at nationals in Colorado Springs. I won my 19th and 20th national titles in the keirin and match sprint, and set an American record for the 200 meters—10.092 seconds. In training, I regularly broke the 200-meter world record. The USA Cycling wanted me to go for the mark, officially. But I remembered my 500-meter world record and the disappointing '98 worlds that followed. I stayed focused on Sydney.

"Forget it," I told them, with a definitive snarl.

I'm riding faster than at any time in my life, but I'm downright mean. Gil says I'm in kill mode. During national team practices, I regularly hook and chop my teammates, just to remind them, and myself, that I'm number one.

I've become the worst, to become the best.

· · · · · · · · ·

I can hear the roar of the motorcycle's exhaust pipes miles before I even reach the Brisbane velodrome. Gil is warming up the engine for a motor-pacing session on the outdoor track, and the sound of the muffler echoes off the concrete banking. The motorcycle burps and whines as Gil revs the engine and shifts gears.

Gil and I have settled into a routine during our stay in Brisbane. He drives to the velodrome with Eddie, my faithful soigneur, and sets up everything I'll need for the day's session—water, food, track bike, all perfectly organized and laid out. I ride my road bike the 15 miles to and from the track as a warm-up and cooldown.

My pre-Olympic training is exactingly measured. I don't expend any energy without a clearly defined purpose. My workouts are like a switch, flipping on and off. Every effort on the bike is made at full throttle. I don't touch weights or chance sparring with other riders. Properly preparing simply means maintaining my form and my patience. Waiting for the racing to start proves more difficult than any workout. I don't sit still well, and my petulance makes everyone tense.

A couple of weeks before the opening ceremony, I fly to Sydney while Gil and Eddie make the 12-hour drive south with all of my equipment. I check into the Olympic Village with the rest of the cycling team, but after a couple of days, I'm done. Few competitors come to the Olympics actually intent on winning a gold medal. Most come for the Olympic experience, the congregation of the world's greatest athletes, the opening ceremony and the chic apparel bearing the interlocking rings.

I'm in Sydney to win, and the lively atmosphere at the Olympic Village is not conducive to that objective. It's past 10 p.m. on my second evening in the Village and the other athletes are up, socializing, making noise.

I call Gil. "I need to get the hell out of here," I say. He's outside the Village in 10 minutes. I move into the apartments the national team rented for the coaching staff, and impose my nightly curfew on everyone staying there—lights out by 9 p.m.

Christian Vande Velde, who's on the pursuit team, is staying at the same apartments as me, and we regularly ride together. Three days before I'm set to compete, we're returning from the velodrome on our road bikes. We're chatting, and I take my hands off the bars to emphasize a point as we ride downhill and into a roundabout at well over 30 miles per hour.

It's the same roundabout we've ridden through a dozen times, but in a momentary lapse of memory, Christian forgets which exit we take. He turns into me and swipes my front wheel. I instantly tumble to the ground. I slide through a traffic-filled intersection, but amazingly don't get hit by a car. It's chilly in Sydney, the start of spring in the Southern Hemisphere, and I'm wearing long leg warmers and a jacket. The excess clothing protects me from the worst of the road rash, but my left knee, the surgically repaired one, starts to swell.

Christian can't believe what he's done. He apologizes profusely. I accept his apology and get back on my bike. Control what you can control. When Gil hears about the accident, he goes nuts. He wants to kill Christian, or at the least, kick his ass. Christian hides out in a nearby room, his door shut tight.

"Don't worry about Christian," I tell Gil, a bag of ice on my knee. "Worry about doing your own job."

In Sydney, Gil's primary task is taking care of my bikes. He's a master mechanic, and the only person I trust to work on my equipment. No one other than Gil touches my bikes. He knows how to give my bikes the Heinz treatment. He respects the sport, and he respects my equipment.

One night, Gil is wrenching on my track bike, a custom-built, carbon-fiber GT, which I'll use to compete in the match sprint. The bike is worth tens of thousands of dollars, and it's painted to match the predominantly blue-and-silver US national team outfits.

Unbeknownst to me, in a brief moment of carelessness, Gil loses his grip on a wrench. It falls from his hand and nicks the bike at the bottom of the frame, near the crankarm. A flake of paint, no larger than the fingernail of a pinky finger, chips off. He freaks out. No racer would notice such a minuscule blemish. No racer except me. I would hang Gil by his ears. I've roughed up a national team mechanic in the past for scratching up one of my bikes.

So Gil gets down on his hands and knees. He scours the floor for the paint flake. Eventually he finds it. Thank God, he says. He superglues the paint chip back into place on the bike, making the accident hardly discernable. Disaster averted. I don't learn about the accident until after Sydney.

· · · · · · · · ·

At the opening ceremony for the Sydney Olympics, 200 stockmen (Australia's cowboy) perform to the theme music of *The Man from Snowy River*. Cliff Meidl, a flat-water kayaker with a severe lower-body disability, carries the flag for the US Olympic team. Cathy Freeman, a 400-meter runner of Aboriginal descent, lights the Olympic flame. By all accounts, it's a touching event.

But I wouldn't know. I'm asleep. I didn't attend the opening and closing ceremonies in Atlanta, and I don't attend the opening ceremony in Sydney. I'm not here to take in the Olympic experience. I'm here to compete against the best in the world, at their best, and beat them.

When the match-sprint tournament finally starts, I exhibit a steely gaze and firmly set jaw, but I'm about to crawl out of my skin with excitement. As the race grew closer and closer, I spent less and less time on the track. I purposefully made myself crave the rush of riding down the banking and hearing the boards hum beneath my wheels.

The Olympic velodrome is brand-new, built to the recent international standard of 250 meters in length with 42-degree banking. The boards are cut from Baltic pine, a soft wood that makes for a slightly slower surface—and favors more powerful riders, like me. Long, arching beams support the metallic gray roof above the completely enclosed track. The bleachers ringing the boards seat nearly 6,000 people. It's named after Dunc Gray, an Australian racer who won gold in the kilometer at the 1932 Games in Los Angeles.

During the course of my career I've rarely qualified first in the flying-200-meter time trial. I tend to get stronger and faster as the match-sprint tournament moves forward. As my opponents fade from the repeated sprint efforts, I gain power. I ride my most blistering 200 meters in the quarterfinal and semifinal rounds.

But in Sydney, I want to come out swinging, throwing body blows, hurting my competition from the first turn of the pedals. The time trial is only 10 seconds long, but aerodynamics will make the difference between qualifying first or second.

I wear Lycra covers over my shoes to limit the resistance caused by the bulky straps. I don an aero helmet with a long fairing that extends down past my shoulders. I run disc wheels on both the front and rear of my bike. I'm an arrow in a bow pulled taut—I'm going to rip the boards right off this track.

Before I ride up onto the banking, I find Christi and the kids in the crowd. They're sitting next to my mom. The moments before my races are the only time I'll see them while I'm in Sydney. I wave. They wave back, excitedly.

It's time to race.

I circle the very top of the track, inches from the hip-high wall that's paneled in blue signs bearing the Olympic logo. I cross the start line, situated directly between turns one and two, for the final time before the clock starts. As I exit turn two, I pull up hard on the pedals, coaxing the bikes big gear into action. I gain momentum down the back straight, turning my massive legs faster, faster. I steady myself with my thick arms.

I stand out of the saddle between turns three and four. I flip the switch on. Suddenly, I'm a laser beam, pointed toward the finish line. I'm accelerating faster than most race cars as I enter the home stretch. The handlebars pull against my shoulders and chest, as if they're trying to squirm loose from the punishment I'm doling out with my body.

I point the front wheel down the banking as I enter the first turn. I cut directly from the top of the track to the timing tape between turns one and two as if I'm riding down a slide. It feels as if someone just put his hand on my back and gave me a big push. I'm flying now, pinned against the black line at the bottom of the track, inches above the apron. I arch my back and bow my arms, making room for my legs to fire up into my chest, then down against the crankarms. *Up, down. Up, down. Up, down. Faster. Faster. Faster.*

In the final turn, I focus on staying smooth, under control. I'm firing my legs, bracing my arms, keeping my head low and aerodynamic. I'm putting out more than 2,300 watts, but my upper back remains nearly motionless, stabilized by my tightened core muscles. I feel the G forces trying to pull my bike up the banking, but I keep the tires pinned against the edge of the track's apron.

I sail through turn four onto the finishing straight, six more pedal strokes from each leg and I'm across the line. Every pedal stroke is the most important of my life, the pedal stroke I've waited 4 years to take. I'm going more than 45 miles per hour when I blow across the line.

I take a huge gulp of air. I wait for the blood to rush back to my head, and my fuzzy vision to clear, then I look at the scoreboard above the screaming rows of spectators.

10.166 seconds.

The time puts me a full 0.1 second in front of the next best qualifiers—Laurent Gané and Florian Rousseau of France—and just 0.03 seconds off of Australian Gary Neiwand's Olympic record from Atlanta.

They don't hand out medals for qualifying, but I allow myself a moment of celebration. I hoist my right arm up above my head, fist clenched. I leave the arm elevated for a brief moment, an exclamation point on an emphatic ride.

I enter the match-sprint tournament seeded first. Jens Fiedler is fourth.

If we both win our first three rounds, we'll meet in the semifinals.

· · · · · · · · ·

I draw my teammate, Marcelo Arrue, in the first round. Marcelo's a
good friend and a great athlete, but I will end his Olympic dream. Racing against Marcelo is like eating one of my own. I don't need to play
games with him; I know I'm faster in a flat-out sprint. I flick down the
banking with a lap and a half to go, overtake Marcelo, and start a delib-
erate charge to the finish.

Marcelo struggles to reach my rear wheel as I sprint down the back
straight on the final lap. The race is over before I exit the final turn. I
roll across the line and raise my arm in the air. I reach back and grab
Marcelo's hand. Good ride, I tell him.

Next.

· · · · · · · · ·

The crowd is whipped into an Aussie fervor as I roll to the start line to
meet my second-round opponent, Sean Eadie. He's a hometown favorite
who lives just 10 miles from the Dunc Gray Velodrome. Eadie trains
here and knows these boards better than the hardwood floors in his own
home. He's Australia's reigning national sprint champion and the country's best shot at a medal. I imagine how I would feel if the Olympics
came to T-Town, and I understand the importance of this race to Eadie.

Everywhere I look, I see gold and blue. The sound of the Aussie
crowd screaming rattles the bleachers and reverberates off the velodrome's metal roof.

"AUSSIE, AUSSIE, AUSSIE!"

"OI, OI, OI!"

"AUSSIE, AUSSIE, AUSSIE!"

"OI, OI, OI!"

Chant. I think. *Keep chanting.*

Gil holds me at the line. After 15 years together, there's still no one else I would want in my corner. There's no one else I would allow in my corner.

We roll off the line. Eadie's tense. I can see it in the way he grips the bar, how he rocks back and forth on the pedals. He's scared of me. I'm a killer on the prowl, a shadow stalking him down a dark alley.

We start at a twitchy walk. I quicken my pace, and Eadie increases his accordingly. He lengthens his stride. He looks back anxiously. I'm still there, coming faster now. Eadie stands and presses the pedals. We're at a brisk trot now. If he can make it to the finish line before I catch him, he's safe. He'll live to ride another day. If he can't outrun me, he's done. He's dead.

One and a half laps to go. Eadie's running now. Running for his life. I'm riding for mine, too. Kill or be killed.

The crowd screams like an audience at a horror movie watching an inevitable massacre: *Run, Eadie, run! Run! The Blade is coming!* And Eadie runs. He runs, until he runs out of gas. We hit the back straight and I move to his right. Then, I swallow him whole. We're in the final turn. I'm beside him. He moves up the banking and bumps me. But I'm unfazed. He bounces off me and back down onto the apron. I move in front of him.

He's dead.

My win sucks the enthusiasm out of the crowd and leaves the large domed ceiling full of sweet silence. *Chant now*, I think.

I raise my arm.

Next.

· · · · · · · · ·

In the quarterfinals, I meet Craig MacLean, who earlier won a surprise medal in the team sprint. He's a Scotsman and took silver as part of the rising British track squad. MacLean is full of bravado and determined to race me aggressively.

Gil presses tight against my body on the start line. He grasps my bike at the seatpost and handlebars and bears my 210-pound frame against his chest on the steeply banked track. I feel his head pressed tightly against my big left biceps.

"Kick his ass," Gil says, and we roll off the line.

MacLean creeps to the front. He eyes me cautiously as I weave up and down the track behind him. He knows I want the front in this match, but he doesn't know if I'm coming underneath him or over the top. I ride up to the railing, and MacLean comes with me. He wants to pin me at the top of the track, to slow down the race, and keep me from pushing him into a long sprint as I did to Eadie.

I swerve at him, feigning a move down the banking. MacLean jumps. We lock eyes. He tries to prove he's not afraid of me, moving even higher up the track, squeezing me against the boards. He tries to prove he's not intimidated, that he can react to any move I throw at him. But he's ridden far too high up the banking.

We enter the fourth turn with just over a lap to go. I flick my bike to the left of MacLean. My front tire misses hitting his rear wheel by just a few millimeters as I shoot down the banking. MacLean scrambles to correct his mistake. He dives down the track and tries to bump me onto the apron. It's a clear foul, but it doesn't matter.

I'm gone. I sprint all out down the finishing straight as the bell clangs, signaling one lap to go. MacLean can't hold my pace. He backs off and prepares for another run at me. But I'm too damn fit and I'm too damn fast for MacLean. He can't catch me. He's a full two bike lengths back as we cross the line.

MacLean's a victim of his own aggression, as I once was.

On the second ride MacLean barely puts up a fight. I drive the pace from behind, and wind up my sprint as the bell clangs one lap to go. I'm beside MacLean on the back straight and past him by the time we enter the third turn. The race is over before we even hit the final run to the line.

MacLean finishes with his hands clasped to the tops of his handlebars, his head tucked down in vanquished shame.

Fiedler's next.

. . . .

This time his helmet is yellow. The helmet is small, and smooth, and the same shade as the yellow in the red, black, and yellow stripes ringing the shoulders of his skinsuit. He wears matching yellow Adidas sunglasses. The dark lenses shield his eyes. A thin, carefully sculpted goatee rings his mouth.

He tightens his lips and forces the breath out of his narrow nose. He beats his chest. His left fist slams against his right pec, *wham*, then his right fist against the left pec, *wham*. He's perhaps the best to ever race this event, a two-time reigning gold medalist with a brilliant tactical awareness and a sprint like a lightning strike. Beating Fiedler at the Olympics presents the biggest challenge of my entire life.

I'm ready.

Savage Garden's "Break Me, Shake Me" blares over the velodrome's speakers, filling the stadium with a thumping drum line. But I don't hear a thing. I shut out everything but me and Fiedler and this track.

Gil grips my bike on the line. I exhale. Grab my handlebars. Nod.

The official blows the whistle. Fiedler takes the lead.

He rides low, just off the apron. I ride close to him, less than a bike length off his rear wheel. My tactic is unusual. Typically the rider in the rear will ride high on the banking, and drop off the top of the track to make a run on their opponent.

Not me. Not today. Four years ago I let Fiedler dictate the pace. I rode up the banking and he blocked me. He kept me from making a run at him. In Sydney, I will control this race from the back. Fiedler's unwillingness to give me the front plays right into my hands.

A half lap in, I start to raise my pace. To maintain his position in the front, Fiedler must raise his own pace. I turn the pedals quicker, quicker still. Fiedler looks back. He sees me coming, just off his rear wheel. He rises from the saddle and throws his bike back and forth. I force him into a near sprint just one lap in.

We hit the back straight with one and a half laps to go, and I come out of the saddle again. I pound the pedals and close within a wheel of Fiedler. He sees me coming and he jumps again, trying to hold me off. We round the fourth turn, coming into the bell lap. We cross the line, already sprinting at over 40 miles per hour. The crowd howls. I'm on Fiedler's heels, and I catch him in the second turn.

I draw beside him on the back straight. He bobs, leveraging every muscle in his body against the pedals. In the fourth turn I reach the back of his right shoulder. Just as in '96, he rides on the red line just outside the sprinter's lane. I know Fiedler will try to hook me, and he does. Fiedler swerves up the track, into me. He tries to knock me back.

Track racing's rules stipulate that I can use my body to protect my space on the track if another rider moves into me. I can use my elbows or my shoulder to keep an opponent clear of my handlebars. In this instance, racing through the turn at damn near 50 miles per hour, I use my head. I lean my shoulder into his torso. I crane my neck, and head-butt him with the top of my helmet, *whack*!

The hit forces Fiedler back down into the sprinter's lane, and clears my path past him. But he still holds a half-wheel advantage on me as we whip through the last turn and onto the finishing straight. I surge with 50 meters to go. Suddenly, I sprint beside him—elbow to elbow.

The lack of oxygen reaching my brain makes everything in my vision a flickering blur. But I can see the line 30 meters away. Twenty meters. Ten. Fiedler and I extend our arms. We tuck our heads—mirror images of each other. We sail across the line.

I win.

I beat Fiedler by a half wheel at the line. This time, there is no photo finish. No official review. No second-guessing. I try to mute my excitement. But this is big. I own the momentum. I jab a fist in the air. I shout into the stadium void. "Yeah!"

Now, I think, *do it again.*

But first, I must maintain my focus. The amount of time between the sprint matches is nothing like the hurried breaks between rounds of boxing. Minutes pass. There's time to warm down, then warm up before the next match. There's time to think, to analyze strategy, to come out for the next match with a new game plan. I'm sure Fiedler is thinking. He lost. He knows he must try something different. My mind flashes back to '96. I lost gold. *I didn't come here for a silver medal.*

We line up for the second sprint. I'm on the inside. Gil holds me. "Kill him," he says. We roll off the line. I'm in front. I ride up to the top of the track, leaving no choice for Fiedler but to drop underneath me. *You want the front*, I think. *Here, take it.*

Fiedler drops into the lead, and immediately I'm pushing him from behind, just as in the last match. He's out of the saddle, flicking the pedals over, gaining speed, and I'm right behind him. I'm in his draft, tucked into his slipstream. The bell clangs. We exit the second turn, onto the back straight. I'm beside him. We enter the third turn, and then the fourth turn. Here comes the hook. Fiedler swerves into me. *Whack!* My head, his torso. My path to pass Fiedler clears, again.

We sprint onto the finishing straight and I'm around him. Fiedler's done, and he knows it. He backs off the pedals. I grit my teeth as I cross the line. I cock my arm, and pump my elbow into my side. *Yes, yes, yes, yes!*

I'm guaranteed a silver medal but silver won't do this time. The Frenchman Florian Rousseau awaits me in the final.

· · · · · · · · ·

Rousseau is a prodigy who fulfilled his promise and then some. He owns 10 Olympic and world championship medals, including a gold medal from these Games in the team sprint. In a country that's synonymous with cycling, Rousseau ranks as one of the most accomplished racers of all time.

And in the match sprint, Rousseau is a silent assassin. He isn't known for his tactical prowess or deft bike handling. He doesn't play games. He isn't an aggressor. I'm told he hates racing me because he doesn't like getting physical. Rousseau wins by riding faster over the last lap of a match sprint than anyone else in the world. To beat Rousseau, I must ride the fastest final 200 meters of my life—twice.

Many sprinters perform exaggerated mental preparations on the start line. With a series of heaving breaths and snorts, they transform themselves from mere competitors, into predators. Rousseau's routine is recognized worldwide. His porcelain-smooth skin draws tight across his face as he flares his nostrils and widens his eyes. He clenches his teeth as if he's ripping into a tough steak. Over a series of inhalations, Rousseau's eyes grow wider and wider, until they're nearly bulging from his skull.

Me, I look as if I could care less. During the '99 season I completely changed my start line routine, a mental preparation similar to a pitcher's wind up, or a basketball player's movements on the free throw line. I don't strut and prance like a fighting cock thrown into a pit. I'm ready to throw down whenever, wherever. As Rousseau performs his interpretive dance on the start line, I sit stoically on my bike, a look of sincere boredom on my face. I take a handful of deep breaths, roll my shoulders, and stare off into space. I always make sure I'm the last rider to grab my handlebars.

I wait for Rousseau to reach down for his drops. Then I count backward for 10 seconds, 10, 9, 8, . . . before grabbing my own handlebars.

I look over at Rousseau and stare him directly in the eye. *Let's fucking race*, I think. Rousseau grabs his handlebars. The official blows the whistle. *You first*, I think.

Rousseau rolls into the lead.

He rides at a measured pace at the bottom of the track. No games. No tricks. We'll just ride as fast as we can ride. I sit behind Rousseau, a bike length off his back wheel. One lap goes by, then two. The bell clangs. Rousseau rises from the saddle. I stand on my pedals. He's going now, and I'm coming.

I'm at Rousseau's wheel by the start of the second turn. I'm in his draft. One, two, three pedal strokes and I'm beside him. One, two, three pedal strokes and I'm a half-wheel in front of him. We enter the third turn, our thick arms braced against our bars, our legs firing with every muscle fiber we can muster.

We're riding for Olympic gold. I'm riding for my life.

We exit the fourth turn and Rousseau can't hold the pace. He sits up. I sail in front of him. I win the first sprint. My mom jumps out of her seat in the stands. I can hear her scream. She puts her hands against her cheeks, and tears stream over her fingers.

I'm no gold medalist yet, though. Rousseau regularly beats competitors in three sprints, wearing them down with his stamina. I can't discount him.

Between rides I go back to the US national team cabin. It's full of supposed cycling dignitaries, USA Cycling and friends of USA Cycling who want a behind-the-scenes look at the action. I want a sterile environment. Clear the cabin, I tell Gil and Eddie. They turn to the USA Cycling officials. I'm sorry, Gil says, but you need to leave, now.

It's just the three of us, me and my team. Gil barks encouragement at me. He won't let me forget that I'm a champion, that I've tortured myself for 4 years for this moment. He knows intimately how my loss in Atlanta haunted me. Three more laps to redemption.

I look over at Rousseau's cabin. He's seated, a wet, white towel draped over his bowed head. "The white flag's out. He's surrendering," Gil shouts at me. "He's done. Go out there and finish him."

We line up. Rousseau performs his prerace histrionics. I calmly reach down and tighten the straps, imprisoning my feet in the pedals. One strap runs across my toes, one strap runs across my arch. I pull on the straps until I feel the bones in my feet compressing. I sit up on the saddle. Hands on my hips. My chest rises up and down as I stare off into space. I clear my mind of everything but me and this track and this man to my left whom I'm about to execute, swiftly and decisively.

The whistle blows. I'm in the lead. I ride up to the top of the banking, along the rail, my head craned over my left shoulder, tempting Rousseau to come through underneath me. At the start of the second lap, he does. He races down to the bottom of the track, and I'm on him, chasing him.

Rousseau looks back, I'm three bike lengths behind. He thinks he has me. He crosses the finish line. One lap to go. The crowd is on their feet. Screaming. My mom is screaming. Christi is jumping up and down, holding Devon tight to her hip with one arm and pumping her delicate fist in the air with the other. Rousseau is sprinting. If I want to win a gold medal, I must catch Rousseau and pass him within the next 250 meters.

My eyes lock on Rousseau's rear wheel; my legs fire. This is my ninth all-out sprint in the past day and a half. A rapture of pain overwhelms my entire body. But it's quickly replaced by an adrenaline torrent. I'm sprinting on determination, on heart, on my deep will to win, and on my hatred of losing. Rousseau is sprinting more than 42 miles per hour, and I must ride 45 miles per hour to catch him. So I do. I'm at his rear wheel in the second turn. I'm beside him on the back straight.

He doesn't swerve. He doesn't hook me. He dares me to ride his pace for as long as he can. But I ride faster. We enter the third turn and Rousseau gives up. We exit the fourth turn, and the second-best sprinter in the world simply stops sprinting. Rousseau bows his head in defeat.

I celebrate on my way to the finish line.

I'm an Olympic champion.

. . . .

A feeling of elation overcomes me. I raise my arms and flex every muscle in my upper body. I just won the biggest gamble of my life. Four years of sacrifice, with no guarantee of success. I soak in the sound of the applause-filled velodrome, and the feeling of me, alone, circling the track as a gold medalist. I want to make sure I can remember this moment for as long as I live.

Then, just as quickly as the elation came, a feeling of relief takes its place. I never knew how much pressure I was under, until the pressure is lifted. Every muscle in my body relaxes simultaneously, as if a giant wave just washed over me, leaving the demons of my loss in Atlanta in its wake. My shoulders slump. My lower back loosens. I pull open the straps holding my shoes in the pedals. I arch my feet. I wiggle my toes.

I look to my left and see Gil running along the apron, leaping up and down. I ride over to Christi and the kids and my mom. We huddle together and I squeeze them tight. I kiss all of them. Tyler squirms. Then, I let them go and pick up my bike. I lift it over my head and let out a primal scream, as if I'm expelling the final vestiges of Atlanta from inside me.

Back in the national team cabin, preparing for the podium presentation, my emotions nearly overcome me. I grab a white towel and drape it over the back of my head. I feel my eyes welling with water. *I did it. I did it*, I think. But I won't let myself cry, not even now. Tears are weak, I'm told.

The medal ceremony starts. I take my place on the highest step. Rousseau stands to my right, Fiedler to my left. A thick medal disc, made with Australian gold, is slipped over my neck. The greatest song in the world, the US national anthem, comes to life over the loudspeakers. I bow my head and think about the path that led me here, and all the people who guided me along the way.

After the medal ceremony, someone hands me an American flag. I ride another victory lap. I wave the flag above my head. Six thousand people stand and clap and cheer for me. But they're cheering for me alone, and I didn't win a gold medal by myself. I stop in front of my family again. I lift Tyler up like a lion carrying a cub. He's a scrawny 5-year-old—a beautiful, blond little boy. He wraps his arms around my neck and clings tight as I roll back down the banking.

"Look at all the people," I tell Tyler.

He turns his head toward the stands, and his blue eyes are wide.

"Wave," I say.

He lifts his tiny arm, decorated with a temporary American flag tattoo, and throws it in the air. He's a showman, just like me, just like his great-great-grandfather. Tyler waves his hand vigorously, a cheek-wide smile on his face. The crowd cheers even more loudly.

· · · · · · · · ·

A day later I line up for the keirin final. I'm the favorite, the rider everyone will work together to beat. Rousseau and Fiedler roll up to the start with their teammates, Magné and Jan Van Eijden, riding in support of them—and against me.

The past 24 hours have flown by in a media blitz. I literally run between interviews with *USA Today*, the *New York Times*, NBC's Katie Couric, and dozens of others. I remain enveloped in a mix of elation and relief.

I lack my killer instinct. I've expended all of my determination in the match sprint. I no longer smell blood. I still smell the fresh roses I held atop the awards podium days earlier as the national anthem played. To me, the match sprint is the most historic and prestigious track race. I got what I came for. The keirin is an afterthought.

The gun sounds and I don't fight for the front as we sprint off the start line. The home favorite, Gary Neiwand takes first wheel. I ride off the back of the group, staying behind the white water. I leave space to make a run over the top of the pack. I eye the group ahead through the clear lenses of my gold-plated Oakleys.

The pace bike pulls off, the riders surge into action, and I'm late to respond. I wind up and jump with one lap to go, but Magné and Van Eijden sit at the back and block my route over the top. They protect their teammates by throwing me sweeping hooks through the final turns. Rousseau wins. Neiwand and Fiedler finish second and third. I'm a disappointing fifth.

But it doesn't bother me, not as it should. Not as it used to.

Christi is more upset than I am. "What were you doing out there?" she scolds.

We fly back to the United States, to my home in the Lehigh Valley, and I'm more content than at any other time in my racing career. I feel free. Free to sleep deeply at night, without asking myself whether I'm doing enough. Free to waste my previously precious energy tossing Tyler high up over my head and tucking Devon into bed on a nightly basis. Free to act like a human, instead of like a robot.

I'm free to live the rest of my life as the Olympic champion.

14

THE IRON MEN
OF CYCLING

AFTER SYDNEY, I wonder, what else? My life as a competitive track cyclist feels complete. I briefly contemplate defending my gold medal in 4 years, in Greece. Then I quickly dismiss the idea. I'll be 33 then. Not past my competitive prime as a bike racer, but more than a decade removed from my first world championship.

Maintaining my position among the top sprinters in the world has worn on my psyche and my body. I'm ready to move on from the sadistic focus required for the one-on-one combat of match sprinting and the grueling regimen of high-intensity training. The sport's horrific high-speed crashes have left my body cobwebbed with deep scars. My torso remains embedded with splinter shards from involuntary slides across wooden track boards.

Moreover, I've collected all of the most prized trophies in track sprinting. I'm no longer driven in the same manner—a determination fueled by my previous failure to secure gold. I don't doubt that I could win gold again, in 2004, but I can't subject Christi, Tyler, and Devon to the same single-minded lifestyle of the previous 4 years.

They made sacrifices for me, now it's time I sacrifice for them. When I'm invited to the White House to have dinner with the president amongst America's other gold medal winners, I have to decline. I had promised Tyler I would attend his school's show and tell that day.

Ever since my second place in the keirin at worlds in 1993, I've received offers to race on the lucrative Japanese keirin circuit. Each year the Japanese invite a handful of foreigners to compete in the races, which serves as a popular betting sport. But year after year I've turned down the money to focus solely on the Olympics. After 2000, I strongly consider racing in Japan. I stand to make tens of thousands of dollars in prize money and appearance fees. But when I find out I won't be allowed to have my family come visit, or fulfill certain sponsor obligations, I can the idea.

I still yearn to test myself against other athletes, but I need a new challenge. An athletic ambition that will also let me be a champion father to my children—not an absentee dad. I decide to become an endurance cyclist. I will race on the road and in mass-start track events. I understand the odds are against me. The transformation to road racing and endurance track cycling is akin to a 100-meter runner taking on marathoners. In the modern era, no Olympic champion track sprinter has successfully transitioned to endurance events.

But my decision isn't without personal precedent. I grew up entering any race I could find. As a kid, I competed in long points races on the track with regularity. I surprised the local cycling community when I won the junior state road race on a bumpy circuit around the Rodale Institute's organic farm. But I've never doubted my own ability to perform in road races and endurance track events. Even during my run toward the Atlanta and Sydney Olympics, I occasionally competed in long, mass-start track races and frequently outperformed the endurance specialists.

My big aerobic engine defined my style as a match sprinter. I could sprint harder for longer than anyone else in the world. Then do it again, and again. I didn't tire during the course of a match-sprint tournament—rather, I got stronger.

Criterium racing dominates the US cycling scene, and with my gold medal–winning sprint, I aim to get a slice of the action. The criteriums in the US are held on closed circuits in the heart of major cities across the country. The race courses range from a half-mile to 2 miles around with tight, technical turns. They last for as long as 60 miles, sometimes as many as 100 laps, and frequently draw thousands of screaming spectators. The showman in me longs to win a big race on the domestic crit racing circuit. I view a career as a domestic road racer as my reward for all those lonely hours on the velodrome.

I'm also intrigued by the European six-day races. I've attended many six-days as a complement to the main event. Now, I want to compete as the primary attraction.

I figure that with a good winter of base training to prepare for a season on the road, I'll start winning handfuls of big events in my new racing discipline.

I'm an Olympic champion. How hard could crit racing be?

· · · · · · · · ·

In 2001, I sign a pro road-racing contract with Mercury-Viatel. The team contains a number of top US and European pros and is hoping to earn a spot in the Tour de France, an event that ranks just below the Olympics and soccer's World Cup in terms of international exposure. My primary job within the team is to get results on the domestic criterium scene and provide the sponsor's exposure within the United States.

Bringing exposure to the team isn't a problem. The local media covers me in every city I race. I'm a reigning gold medalist, a story-worthy competitor. I sign scores of autographs and make excited commentary for race announcers at big events. I'm worth every cent Mercury-Viatel pays me because of my Olympic panache.

But I struggle to get results. I don't even crack the top 30 in my first few national-level races. My handling skills and ability to jostle for position isn't an issue. But I lack the strength required to keep myself at the front of the pack toward the end of the race. Sprinting at the end of a 60-mile race proves entirely different than after a few laps around the velodrome. I'm also unaccustomed to relying on teammates, and I don't trust them to guide me into position at the end of a race.

I quickly learn the head of the race in the last few laps of a criterium is a tiny club of elite sprinters, and they don't give a warm welcome to newcomers. My gold medal doesn't automatically earn me a clear shot to unleash my powerful sprint in sight of the line. All of the attention I garner as an Olympic champion makes me seem entitled, and gives my competitors extra motivation to keep me from winning.

I want my foray into professional road racing to serve as more than an extended victory lap from Sydney. I want to win in front of thousands of cheering fans. And to do so, just as with everything I've done on the bike, I'll have to earn it.

The intensity of my training for road racing pales in comparison to my track work, but that doesn't mean it's not daunting. Although I put in as much as 50 hours a week at the gym and on the track during my training for the Olympics, I now sometimes spend up to 30 hours a week on my bike. I start each New Year's Day by riding 100 miles. I gather the local road racers for a big, cold group ride. If it's snowing, I set up rows of stationary trainers at the local gym, and we do the 100-mile ride indoors.

Over time, I physically adapt to the demands of road racing and garner respect from my competitors. I become strong enough to ride at the front of the race, and other racers quickly learn if they don't let me go where I want, I'll make the space myself—often with disastrous results for them.

· · · · · · · · ·

In August of 2003, I line up beside the best criterium racers in the world for the New York City Cycling Championship. I'm now riding for Navigators Insurance, one of the top US-based pro teams. My former team, Mercury-Viatel, imploded in 2001 after it wasn't selected to compete in the Tour de France.

The New York City race takes place in the heart of the financial district, right down Wall Street. The 1.2-mile loop contains eight turns and a 50-foot section of rough cobblestones. We'll do 50 laps of the course, for 60 miles total. The race's prize purse tops $40,000. I circled the race date on my calendar at the start of the year and trained for it like an Olympic event. It's a race worthy of special devotion, with throngs of fans, live TV coverage, and celebrities like Jerry Seinfeld hovering around the start line.

I aim to win.

Threatening dark clouds hover above the Manhattan skyscrapers. As the barometric pressure drops, the old creases in my previously fractured kneecap, heel, and ribs begin to ache. A storm is coming, and when it does, chaos will rain down on the twitchy pack of a hundred-plus pro riders. "Stay near the front," Ed Beamon, my current team director, implores before the start.

I get my obligatory call to the line. "Olympic gold medalist, The Blade, Marty Nothstein . . .," the announcer drawls. Racers mired at the back of the big bunch roll their eyes. That muscle-bound track sprinter can't win a big crit, they snipe.

With everyone uncertain about the weather, the race starts hard from the gun. Thirty minutes in, I make a large split of 20 riders. I have two teammates in the front group with me. We like our odds of winning, and help drive the break. We tow the group into the winds whipping through the concrete canyons made by the giant buildings, and soon build a 40-second gap over the chasing field of racers behind us.

Tens of thousands of fans line the barricades ringing the course. It feels as if I'm riding through a tunnel of sound as we fly down the long finishing straightaway at speeds of more than 35 miles per hour. The race seems effortless. A sense of invincibility envelops me. When a rider from the US Postal Service team, Antonio Cruz, attacks near the end of the race, I go with him.

We're joined by a Spanish pro, José Azevedo, who just finished the

Tour de France. The three of us ride together smoothly for four laps, building a 15-second advantage over the chase group. Beamon anxiously reminds me not to spend all my bullets before the finish. "Relax, relax, relax," he yells into the race radio.

With 10 laps to go, we're reabsorbed by the main breakaway, now whittled down to 16 riders. Rain drops start to dot my arms. A deluge is coming. At two laps to go, a thin film of water covers the streets, making the corners perilously slick. But I make it to the final lap without any incidents, perfectly positioned to win.

In the final 500 meters, my teammate, an Italian named Siro Camponogara, attacks, forcing the Saturn team to chase. I jump on the wheel of Saturn's sprinter, Victor Rapinski, who is a former junior world champion on the track. Rapinski takes me to the final 100 meters, where I let loose.

It's not even close.

I cross the line alone, my right arm raised, my fist tightened.

Moments after the rest of the field finishes, the sky opens up. The rain comes down in droves. I feel renewed. I'm a champion again.

I'm home in the Lehigh Valley that same night, after my win in New York City. It's dark out, and Tyler and Devon are already in bed. I slip into their rooms while they sleep. They're perfect, angelic little kids. I kiss Tyler goodnight.

Then, as I kiss Devon goodnight, she wakes up.

"I love you, Dad," she says. She's three and a half. My heart melts.

"I love you too, Devon," I say. "I'll see you in the morning."

· · · · · · · · ·

My longest separations from Tyler and Devon come during the winter, when I head to Europe to compete on the six-day circuit. Though it pains me to leave the kids behind, I'm instinctively drawn to the six-day scene. The racing style is its own discipline within the bike racing world—one part track race and one part stage race, with a dash of WWF-style showmanship and circus-like atmosphere.

The six-days take place from October through February, and the circuit visits all of Europe's most cycling-crazy cities, including Amsterdam, Berlin, Munich, and Copenhagen. The European enthusiasm for six-day races is equivalent to college basketball's March Madness in the United States. The races take place inside the largest arena in each city with a velodrome often specially constructed in advance of the event. Tens of thousands of fans pack the stadium, clapping along to Europe's latest techno hits. Laser-light shows flash across the track between races.

We race from roughly 7 p.m. to 1 a.m. for 6 consecutive days. Each evening is broken up into various track events, with the Madison races serving as the most important events every night. The two-man Madison teams accumulate points by either lapping the field, or winning the sprints held every few laps. The team with the biggest overall lead after the 6 nights of racing wins the entire six-day. In addition to the Madisons, the racers also compete in flying-lap and elimination races (where the last rider on each lap is pulled from the pack).

The six-day schedule is grueling. I accumulate as many as 100 miles each night, from competing in at least a dozen all-out races. Each evening, after the racing ends, I sit at a communal dinner table with my fellow racers, including Tour de France stars like Erik Zabel, Stuart O'Grady, and Bradley Wiggans. We shovel food into our mouths at 2 a.m. and talk about the inhumanity of the six-day format.

I look into the sunken eyes of these hardened Euro pros and listen to them compare the six-day experience to a 3-week stage race like the Tour de France. At the Tour, they tell me, you can at least sit comfortably in the peloton for 5 hours before having to sprint. They explain there are days in the Tour when you ride steadily in the *grupetto*, far behind the action at the front of the race, and get a chance to rest. But at the six-days, the racing intensity is nearly full throttle for the whole evening.

In a large pack on the open road, you can get lost among the sea of riders. Inside the velodrome, there is no place to hide. The racing takes place under a microscope. If you're suffering, everyone will know.

Unlike the Tour, which allows for a day of rest at the end of each week, the six-day races are frequently scheduled back-to-back. Often, we travel the morning after a six-day race finishes, and start another the very next day. After weeks on end of the nonstop track racing, the competitors start to wear down.

The rest of the world views the six-day racers as the iron men of cycling. Despite terrible crashes and ghastly injuries, the races always continue. I witness an up-and-coming road sprinter named Mark Cavendish lying in a pool of blood in Dortmund, Germany, then watch as he goes on to race in Munich the very next day. Many of the tracks we race on are temporary, with bumpy seams that cause horrific saddle sores. The soigneurs brew their own chamois creams, which they refer to as "fat," to try to ease the pain emanating from each racer's crotch. One day, I watch a soigneur apply the salve to a racer's perineum that is so shredded it looks like a vagina.

The late nights make me into a vampire. I rely heavily on sleeping pills to keep the sunlight flooding in through the hotel-room windows from waking me. But I still roll in bed during the early-morning hours, trying to come down from the high of racing in front of thousands of roaring fans. During the six-days, I experience some of the loneliest moments of my life, isolated by language barriers and living in a fog of near-constant fatigue.

Not everything about the six-day is as it might appear to the thousands of inebriated spectators who fill the velodrome's stands, either. On the final night of each six-day, the race organizer meets with the racers for a discussion. The organizer and racers collectively determine the finishing positions of each team based on their current standing in the overall points, their status with the fans, and the amount of cash their sponsor is funneling into the event. If the group can't form a consensus, the race organizer simply tells the racers how the evening will play out. ·

Nearly every six-day race comes down to the final point sprint on the final night of racing. The teams agree to abide by this fixed system because they sign their contract for each six-day well before the racing begins. Whether they finish first or last, the payment doesn't change. The final placing is simply for pride and prestige—which is more important than anything.

Even though the racers know the six-day will come to a predetermined end, the speeds on the track are no less intense. In essence, we're just big kids zipping around on our bikes, and our childish play-fights often unravel into full-on brawls. The moment one rider launches a scintillating attack, the field flies into a tornado of action for laps on end, each team trying to prove themselves the alpha racers.

At the start of each six-day, a veteran racer is nominated as "the Chief" (though the Euros terribly mispronounce this as "the Chef"). The Chief maintains control of the various Madison races and makes sure everyone ultimately abides by the race organizer's wishes. Disobeying the Chief's orders during a Madison can prove costly in terms of future six-day invites and contract negotiations.

· · · · · · · · ·

In 2001 I sign contracts to compete in a half dozen six-day races. My partner for the first six-day is arranged by the race's promoter, Patrick Sercu. Sercu teams me with a talented American endurance rider, with whom I have an antagonistic history. His personality is the antithesis of mine. When I complain to Sercu, he tells me, "You don't have to marry him, you just have to ride with him." I have to agree with Sercu that on paper, my partner should perform well in the six-day race format.

But once the racing starts, we flounder. My teammate is tentative when aggressive racing is required. And though I'm given deference as an Olympic champion, the other six-day racers don't respect my American teammate. Each night, they purposely make it difficult for us to stay at the front of the race.

The only way I can get a new partner is if my current partner can't race due to injury. So, when my teammate comes down the banking to take a hand sling from me during one of the Madison races, I grab his hand and fling him down onto the track. To the crowd, the crash appears to be an accident, just one of the many mishaps in a Madison.

My partner isn't seriously injured, but I make sure he knows the crash was no mistake. When I see him in our cabin between races, I tell him, "Don't go back out there."

The following evening, I'm teamed with a Frenchman named Robert Sassone. He's a veteran, and former world Madison champion, who knows how to properly sling me into the race. We gain the respect of the other six-day teams. I'm suddenly competitive against the top teams and in the thick of the action each night. I complete my initial six-day race and a slew of following six-day races with relative success.

I also win individual championships in elimination races and flying-lap competitions nearly every evening. I set track records at various velodromes across Europe. Sometimes, I even compete in the sprint tournaments against my old adversaries, like Fiedler, and regularly dust them.

"You're turning into quite the endurance rider," Fiedler coyly tells me during one sprint competition. "Why are you doing this?" he asks.

"Because I enjoy the challenge, and I'm making multiple times what you get paid to sprint," I tell him. "You wouldn't last two laps out here," I say.

In 2002 I partner with one of my best friends, Ryan Oelkers, for the last six-day of the season, in Moscow. I still teasingly remind Ryan that he crashed me during a practice Madison exchange before the '94 world championships. But he's recently redeemed himself.

A year earlier, Ryan carried me to a win in the prestigious Madison Cup at the T-Town velodrome. Competing against a field of top international racers, I was having a bad race and was blown coming into the final lap. I gave Ryan a last-second hand sling into the action. He came through big, finishing in the top three in the final point sprint of the night, and securing our overall victory.

In Moscow, I'm coming into my own as an endurance racer and am in some of my best form since Sydney. Ryan's trained his ass off to get ready for Moscow, too. During the fall, we would ride the Derby in T-Town, then I would ride with him back toward his home in Philly, before turning around and coming back to the Lehigh Valley. In Moscow, Ryan just needs to keep us in the mix during the Madison races and give me some brief moments of relief between the point sprints.

He struggles at times, but relies on his considerable toughness to get him through the races. When the race organizer sits down with the various teams on the final night, I lobby vocally for Ryan and me to win. The two top teams on the six-day circuit skipped Moscow, and the Russians, the home favorites, aren't anywhere near the top of the rankings. I've proven myself a consistent racer, the strongest individual rider at the six-day, and a worthy winner. We're currently sitting in second overall, just a lap down on the leaders. "Give us the victory," I implore.

But Ryan's an unknown. Some of the veteran racers question his ability to come through on the final night. If he lags, we won't put on a show worthy of a first-place six-day team for the audience. Ryan won't falter, I promise. The group agrees—we'll finish first overall. We'll still have to dig deep to regain the lap and take the lead. The other teams won't take it easy on us. But if we can maintain the pace at the front, and don't crash out, we'll become the first Americans to win a European six-day in half a century. Make one mistake, and the other teams will surely flick us, stealing the win for themselves.

The final evening of the Moscow six-day starts with a parade. Ryan and I ride side by side in the row of 16 teams, which makes for a total of 32 riders on the tight track. We smile and salute the crowd, excited for our big night. We look dapper in our six-day jerseys, Stars-and-Stripes silk tunics bearing our numbers on the sleeves and our team's sponsor on the chest. I've lost 25 pounds since I switched to endurance racing and stopped my heavy-weight-lifting regimen. The lean muscles of my new physique ripple under the spotlights shining from above the track.

As we casually circle the steep track, the rider in front of Ryan decides to take off his warm-up jacket. The rider wants to show off his jersey as he approaches the front of the parade. Ryan watches the rider remove both his hands from the bars and try to throw the jacket down to his soigneur standing at the apron. He sees the rider's front wheel begin to wobble, and then he looks on in disbelief as the rider sprawls across the boards in front of him.

Ryan has nowhere to go. He flips over the fallen rider in front of him and slides down to the apron at the bottom of the track. A massive hematoma forms under his shorts, making it look as if he has sprouted a third ass cheek.

But we can't let anyone know that he's hurt. If the other teams see a chink in our armor, they'll surely argue we don't deserve the win.

"You okay?" I ask Ryan.

"Yeah," he says. Only a broken bone could stop him from racing tonight.

The racing starts and Ryan shuts out the pain in his hip. He keeps us in the thick of the action when I need relief. Then, we fumble an exchange during one of the Madison races. I hit the track hard myself. As I slide across the boards, skin burns off the side of my body. Blood stains my fine silk jersey. But I get up and keep racing. We don't lose any ground on the front pack.

As the night winds to a close, we gain back a lap on the leaders. Then, as planned, I take the final sprint of the evening, and secure our victory. The vodka-infused fans go nuts. We're showered with flowers and trophies at the awards celebration.

I go on to compete with various other partners in 28 six-day races over the next 4 years, more than any other American in the modern era. I finish third at six-day races in Ghent, Belgium, and Stuttgart, Germany. But Moscow remains my only win.

15

HOME—T-TOWN

IN THE FALL of 2005 I'm presented with an opportunity to give back to the sport that gave me everything. The T-Town velodrome offers me a part-time position as an assistant director at the track.

I grew up at the velodrome and am thrilled to now return as an employee. I gladly accept. The velodrome is my second home: The track served as my childhood playground; the lush, green infield grass, an immaculate front lawn; the concession stand, an always-stocked pantry; and the bleachers, an expansive living room seating my extended family—the fans.

Within the confines of the T-Town velodrome, I learned lessons about both bike racing and life. I celebrated many of my most memorable victories at T-Town. I exchanged heated words and shared hugs. I morphed from a boy into a man, and then into an adult, and I'm eager to lead other racers along the path I followed. My cycling career has come full circle. I've gone from being a T-Town developmental program rider, to an Olympic champion, to a track director.

Over the next year, I wean myself away from life as a professional cyclist while working on various projects for the track. I help coordinate the developmental programs for T-Town and proudly become the namesake for the Marty Nothstein Bicycle Racing League, a program that provides the same support, instruction, and inspiration that I received growing up.

I'm also reunited with Erv, who retired in 2001 after his own foray into road racing, when he is hired as executive director of the velodrome.

Then, on August 26, 2006, I decide to bring the final chapter of my life as a professional bike racer to a close. I retire. I end my career as the most decorated American track cyclist of all time, after more than 15 years at the highest level of the sport. I'm widely regarded as one of the best sprinters, ever, to ride the boards.

I leave cycling with 35 national championships, four Pan-Am Games gold medals, three world championship titles, and hundreds of other victories in top international and domestic races. During my career, I set multiple national, world, and Olympic records. And while I look back on my extensive racing résumé with reverence, I would easily trade in every accolade I ever earned, including my Olympic silver medal, for the gold I won in Sydney.

The journey from Atlanta to Sydney—the disappointment of the silver medal and the resulting Olympic victory—remains the defining moment of my life as an athlete.

· · · · · · · · ·

Fittingly, my retirement ceremony takes place at T-Town on a Friday night. I look up at the bleachers surrounding the velodrome and a warm sense of nostalgia courses through me. The seats are filled to capacity with spectators, people who've come to send me off. During a break in the racing, Erv steps up to a microphone and reads a speech to the crowd.

He says:

> Tonight we send off into the armchair of retirement one of America's all-time greatest cyclists. Though I am now privileged and honored to be working alongside one of America's greatest athletes at

the Lehigh Valley Velodrome, I will miss his intensity and passion on the bike.

There was nothing like a match-sprint round with Nothstein in the mix.

It was always exciting to watch Marty race—whether at a world championships with the season on the line or at a local event with little more than pride riding on the outcome. Marty always gave his best and never failed to impress, especially here on his hometown track, the Lehigh Valley Velodrome.

He is a man truly worthy of being an Olympic champion. I remember clearly the moment he shifted gears and made the commitment to win the 2000 Olympic Games in Sydney. A dramatic change came over Marty that summer day in Atlanta; a fire lit in his eye, and—I can still hear it today—he said in an unwavering voice that he would not lose again in 4 years.

Marty held true to that commitment, winning the most coveted trophy in sports: an Olympic gold medal. He did it with panache, passion, and an unmatched will to succeed, not losing a single ride in one of the most dominant performances in Olympic cycling history.

However, as awesome as his gold medal performance was, to this day, the one thing that impresses me more about Marty Nothstein is his unwavering commitment to T-Town and the Lehigh Valley Velodrome. He rarely left the Valley, even during a cold Pennsylvania winter. He was right here, plugging away, "Rocky Balboa"–style, waiting for his turn to win it all. He loved being here, training using his local resources, and proving that anything one needed to succeed was right here in the Valley.

Marty truly epitomizes the best "end result" of the Lehigh Valley Velodrome and its developmental programs. We can't thank him enough for the memories and accomplishments throughout the years and for the support that he's shown his home track.

Marty, on behalf of the Lehigh Valley Velodrome, we honor you by permanently stamping your name on the premises, as dedicated in a street named in your honor. I present to you "Marty Nothstein Way," a street that will encompass the semicircular road that comes off Mosser Road and passes right in front of the entranceway to the track you helped make famous. Congratulations Marty.

· · · · · · · · ·

Now, nearly every day, I get up before dawn and drive my beat-up Ford F-250 pickup truck down the hill from my home, 10 minutes to the Valley Preferred Cycling Center (the title sponsor of the T-Town track). I pull into Marty Nothstein Way, park in the asphalt lot between the old red barn and the entrance to the track, and walk into the small administrative building that houses my office.

In 2008, Erv resigned as executive director of the velodrome, and I was selected to fill his position. Since then, I've made running the velodrome my new Olympic challenge. As the executive director at T-Town, my own success is now dependent upon the success of the track. My passion for cycling drives me. I approach each day at the office with the same tenacity and attention to detail that I used to give my marathon weight-lifting sessions.

One day, I'm securing a big corporate sponsorship for the velodrome. Another day, I'm doing the dirty work no one else wants to do, such as plunging a clogged toilet. There's always some task that needs my attention, or a person that needs my time. I never stop moving. I don't like to sit still.

The last two seasons of Friday night racing were among the best attended and most profitable in the track's existence. The numerous developmental programs are overflowing with exuberant kids, including my own daughter, Devon, who won the national championship for the girls 10 to 12 age group in 2010. Even the Tuesday night Pro-Am racing draws a sizeable, enthusiastic crowd. (It helps that admission is free, a local craft beer costs only three bucks, and the concession stand serves organic hamburgers and fries.)

From well before the sun rises to the dark hours of the evening, the velodrome hums with people enjoying the pure pleasure of riding a bicycle on a banked oval. The Valley Preferred Cycling Center offers early-morning cycling classes for adults, open training sessions in the afternoons, and nightly competitions 7 days a week—from 5-year-old kids racing in the PeeWee Peddlers on their BMX bikes to the employees of local businesses prepping for the rivalry-filled Corporate Challenge. My talented, passionate, and hardworking staff somehow makes sure all this activity flows smoothly during the course of each season.

· · · · · · · · ·

In the fall of 2011, I'm inducted into the US Bicycling Hall of Fame. I honestly nearly forgot that 5 years had passed since my retirement, the minimum requirement for eligibility. I make it into the Hall of Fame my first time on the ballot—a great honor. I travel to California for the induction ceremony.

The US Bicycling Hall of Fame recently moved to Davis, California, one of the nation's best cycling cities. It previously sat in a small storefront on the finishing strip of the country's longest running criterium in Somerville, New Jersey. The new building is situated in Davis's Central Park, among delicately landscaped gardens.

Plaques and memorabilia honoring the sport's illustrious past line the walls inside the 8,000-square-foot Hall of Fame. I read the bios of champions such as A. A. Zimmerman, who won the very first match-sprint world championship in 1893; the incomparable Major Taylor; and Frank

Kramer, whose photo hangs on the wall of my office back in T-Town. Twenty years before me, in 1991, Bob Rodale was inducted into the Hall of Fame as a contributor to the sport, specifically for his construction of a world-class velodrome in a vacant field in Trexlertown, Pennsylvania.

I look at the plaque with my name on it and think of the thousands of miles ridden and the tons of weight lifted; my blood, running with sweat across the surface of my smoothly shaved skin; the relationships that were either strengthened through my competitive determination or swept aside like so many opponents. I look at my plaque and think of the steadfast pursuit, and ultimate attainment, of a singular goal under asphyxiating pressure.

I look at my plaque, hanging among the pantheon of cycling's greatest champions, and I think, *shit, that was one hell of a ride.*

· · · · · · · · ·

Back in T-Town, on one of the final Tuesday night Pro-Ams of the racing season, three generations of Nothsteins show up at the track—a common occurrence when the weather's nice and Tyler's racing. Tyler is a teenager now and making his own way through the track cycling ranks. So far as I can tell, he's truly enjoying the journey.

My dad positions himself on a stool at turn four, a stately figure peering over the railing. The rest of my family, including my mom and Christi's dad, who remains a fervent racing fan, congregate nearby. Christi drifts through the crowd, mingling with old friends as she keeps one eye on Devon and the other on the action on the track.

For Christi and me, my retirement, and the redefining of our roles as parents and partners, proved initially rocky. But we've since settled into our post-Olympic life as a cohesive family, with Christi remaining the consummate, positive force behind the scenes. (I do, however, make my own cereal these days. Thank-you very much.)

Gil hangs out at the track near where he and Whitehead used to drink beer and cheer for me on Tuesday nights. But now, Gil reserves Tuesday evenings to spend time with his own 11-year-old son, Joey. They eat monstrous Italian hoagies and shout for Tyler (long and lanky, he's nicknamed Bones) as he battles men twice his age.

Though Gil counts his unwavering allegiance to helping me win gold as one of his life's greatest achievements, he never gave up his own competitive ambitions. In the fall of 2011, he traveled to Manchester, England, to compete in the masters world championships. He won the match sprint in the 55 to 59 age category and added another world title to the junior world title he won 37 years earlier. Gil celebrated so wildly after his win in Manchester, the officials gave him a warning.

Whitehead planned an end-of-season trip to T-Town, he surely would have loved watching Tyler race, but he never made it. He passed away unexpectedly during the summer of 2011. Whitehead's death affected me deeply, as if I lost a piece of my childhood along with him. As my racing career progressed, Whitehead morphed from a mentor to a competitor, and then to a member of my team. He remained part of a close circle of people I trusted and felt comfortable around during the height of my gold medal push. He intrinsically understood the demons I battled, because he undoubtedly fought his own.

The velodrome staff commemorated Whitehead with a special evening at the T-Town track, a place where he was both reviled and revered—and will forever remain known as the Outlaw. Though he never shied away from confrontation (and was, admittedly, often responsible for the altercations), most anyone who spent time with Whitehead counted him as a great friend, and nearly everyone who watched him race agrees: He was one of the best damn bike racers they ever saw.

Heinz still lives across the street from my parents' old home and remains a fixture at the track. On the rare occasion that I jump into a local race with Tyler, I hear Heinz yelling, "Move up, Blade." Mike passed away in 2009. Right up until the end, he remained a regular spectator on Friday nights and was instrumental in getting handicap access at the T-Town track. Even while working as the track's assistant director, I continued to rely on his intelligent bike-racing perspective. Similar to Whitehead's death, losing Mike pained me. He was so instrumental to my early life. I will miss him.

In his honor, I created the Mike Walter Madison, a tribute to the event he excelled in as a racer. The race, which takes place at T-Town every year, is 100 laps with point sprints every 10 laps. It's the kind of race Mike would've loved, long and hard, and respectful of the sport's illustrious history.

As the Tuesday night Pro-Am winds to an end, my attention turns to the track. Tyler made it to the finals of the amateur keirin in his first attempt at the event. On his way to the start area, he looks for his mom and his sister. He smiles at his grandpa. I find Tyler before he lines up. I place my hand on his shoulder. I look him the eyes. "Don't try to be the next Marty Nothstein," I say. "Become your own bike racer." He nods.

Gil holds Tyler at the line, just as he held me. "Get 'em, kid," Gil whispers in Tyler's ear.

The start gun fires. The racers surge behind the motor. Tyler jockeys for position. The laps tick by, one after another. The motor peels off the track. Tyler stays out of the scrum, in front of the white water, out of the rough stuff. One lap to go. The bell rings. The tightly bunched pack flies down the back straight. Tyler sits second wheel, spinning faster than everyone else on his junior gears, perfectly positioned to go for the win. "C'mon Bones!" Gil yells. *Good job Tyler,* I think. The racers whip out of the final turn. They fan across the track, from the apron to the rail, and sprint for the line.

INDEX

An asterisk (*) indicates that photos appear in the photo gallery.